Leningrad:
A Case Study
of Soviet Urban
Government

Map 1
City of Leningrad, Including the Suburbs

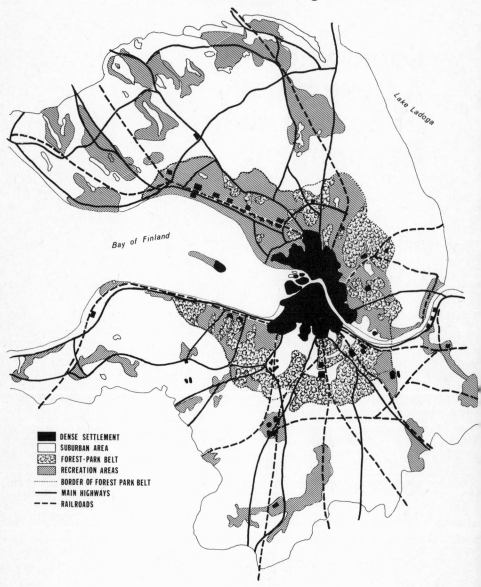

Lake Ladoga

Bay of Finland

DENSE SETTLEMENT
SUBURBAN AREA
FOREST-PARK BELT
RECREATION AREAS
BORDER OF FOREST PARK BELT
MAIN HIGHWAYS
RAILROADS

PRAEGER SPECIAL STUDIES IN
INTERNATIONAL POLITICS AND PUBLIC AFFAIRS

Leningrad:
A Case Study
of Soviet Urban
Government

David T. Cattell

Published in cooperation with the
Institute of Public Administration, New York

FREDERICK A. PRAEGER, Publishers
New York · Washington · London

The purpose of the Praeger Special Studies is to make specialized re-search monographs in U.S. and international economics and politics available to the academic, business, and government communities. For further information, write to the Special Projects Division, Frederick A. Praeger, Publishers, 111 Fourth Avenue, New York, N.Y. 10003.

This book is No. 5 in the series *The International Urban Studies of the Institute of Public Administration, New York*

FREDERICK A. PRAEGER, PUBLISHERS
111 Fourth Avenue, New York, N.Y. 10003, U.S.A.
5, Cromwell Place, London S.W.7, England

Published in the United States of America in 1968
by Frederick A. Praeger, Inc., Publishers

Library of Congress Catalog Card Number: 68-23360

Printed in the United States of America

In Memoriam

JOSEPHINE M. TREDWELL

FOREWORD

This study of Leningrad represents one of a series of similar case studies on urban government prepared under the aegis of the International Urban Studies Project of the Institute of Public Administration, New York.

While IPA applied a uniform research outline to most of the case studies in the series, this research on Leningrad was designed and carried out by Professor Cattell himself. The author has included appropriate data and subject matter to provide for comparability with the other studies in the series. In addition to other case studies, publications of the international project include a comparative volume, <u>The Urban Challenge to Government</u>, by Annmarie H. Walsh (to be published by Frederick A. Praeger, Inc., in 1968).

This work on Leningrad represents a particularly important contribution to knowledge of urban political and administrative systems. Professor Cattell stands out among Western scholars for his experience and concentrated research on Soviet urban government. IPA is most grateful for his participation in the project.

Lyle C. Fitch, President
Institute of Public Administration
New York

PREFACE

The specific purpose of this study on
Leningrad is not to point out universal patterns,
but to deal with the special characteristics and
problems of urban government in the Soviet Union.
Although Leningrad is not a typical Soviet city,
it is the only city--with the exception of Moscow
and, to a lesser extent, Kiev--to which Western
scholars have some access. Furthermore, Soviet
scholars themselves have written more about Leningrad than any other cities except Moscow. Moscow
would have little value as a case study of Soviet
local government because it is the capital of the
U.S.S.R. and the R.S.F.S.R. (its largest republic)
and houses the head offices of a highly centralized
economy.

Leningrad's special position, as this study
demonstrates, points out more poignantly than would
an investigation of a city of lesser importance
some of the basic difficulties and frustrations of
local administrators. The city's privileged position is based on its recognized status as a cultural center almost equal to Moscow and its resulting attractiveness to artists, scholars, and scientists. Second, because of its reputation as a
cosmopolitan city, as the capital of the Russian
empire for 200 years, and as a revolutionary and
socialist center, the population of Leningrad has
developed a fierce loyalty and a sense of community. Third, its civic leaders have held important
positions in the over-all Soviet hierarchy and
have had access to high councils in Moscow. Finally, from the time of the Revolution, the city has
directly controlled a major portion of housing,
retail trade, and even light manufacturing. Hence,
if Leningrad has trouble dealing with the central

bureaucrats, is tightly controlled in its activities, is short of resources, and is frequently at odds with its major industries, it is easy to imagine the frustrations of the more typical urban centers in the U.S.S.R. At the same time, the status of Moscow and Leningrad help in understanding the slow development of culture, welfare, and living standards in most other Soviet cities, which by comparison are not popular places in which to live.

Research for this study was carried out while I was an exchange research scholar at the Universit of Leningrad in 1962 and again in 1966. The main difficulty in conducting research on local government in the Soviet Union is in gaining access to basic information on the operations of local administration. Soviet administrators do not consider government administration at any level to be a matter of direct public concern, and for many years activities even of local governments were classified secret for alleged security reasons. Although there has been some relaxation of security restrictions, published material and case studies on Lenin grad are few compared to Western cities. It is impossible, for example, to get an over-all table of organization for the city or for most of its departments. Most detailed budget figures are still secret and except for a few superficial articles on local Party organization, information on the operations of the Party and on its relations with the local government is not available. By means of interviews with city administrators, continuous perusal of the press, and published resolutions and minutes it was possible to fill in some of the gaps but much of the interaction between departments remains obscure. However, the statistics and information that are available appear to be accurate, and there is no reason to doubt their validity. Thus, for example, all secondary research confirmed the claim that there had been a tremendous expansion of housing and the general welfare of the population.

I would like to express my gratitude to the University of Leningrad for providing me with the

opportunity to do the research on the city of
Leningrad and for arranging interviews with city
administrators. The analysis and conclusions are
mine, and no one at the University of Leningrad is
responsible for them nor would they probably agree
with them. I also wish to express my appreciation
to the Institute of Public Administration and the
Inter-University Committee on Travel Grants who
helped finance the research.

D. T. C.

Los Angeles, California
September, 1967

CONTENTS

LIST OF CHARTS, TABLES, AND MAPS

MAPS

GLOSSARY

All-Union Government

        is the federal government of the Soviet
Union. According to the 1936 Constitu-
tion, it shares sovereign powers with
the governments of the fifteen republics.
Its primary organs are the Supreme Soviet
of the U.S.S.R. and its Presidium, the
All-Union Council of Ministers, and the
Supreme Court of the Soviet Union.

City of Leningrad (Greater Leningrad)

        as decreed by the Supreme Soviet of the
R.S.F.S.R. in 1965 includes the major
population center at the mouth of the
Neva River flowing into the Baltic Sea,
as well as the surrounding suburban and
rural areas and numerous towns. The
region is under the jurisdiction of the
Leningrad City Soviet and is subdivided
into nineteen rayon or district governments.

City Proper of Leningrad

        is composed of the fourteen rayons or
districts that are the city's most
densely populated central areas. The
boundaries of these urban rayons have
been increased gradually.

Dezhurnii

        are the men or women on duty in an en-
tire building or on one floor whose task
it is to supervise maintenance and pro-
tect property.

Druzhini

are citizens recruited to patrol the
streets and public places and to help
the militia maintain public order.

Duma

was the term used before 1917 in Russia
for a parliament or representative
assembly.

Executive Committee

of the city soviet is the committee
elected by the city soviet from among its
members and is composed of the various
heads of administrative departments and
other representatives. It is charged
with the administration of the city and
has authority of the city soviet when it
is not in session.

Glavleningradstroi

is the Chief Management for Housing,
Civil and Industrial Construction in the
city of Leningrad. It is attached to
the Executive Committee of the city but
is responsible primarily to the R.S.F.S.R.
Ministry of Construction.

Gorkom (or Lengorkom)

is the Party committee charged with the
administration of Party organizations in
the city. It is elected by the Communist
Party conference for the city which meets
about every two years, and it has the
authority of the Party conference when
the conference is not in session.

Gosbank

is the state bank centered in Moscow
with branches in all major cities and
towns. It oversees most of the day-to-
day financial transactions of the
economy.

Gosplan

is the State Planning Commission centered
in Moscow but with subordinate committees
attached to the ministers' councils of
the republics and to the executive committees of most local government units.

Gostroi

is the State Committee for Construction
of the U.S.S.R. Council of Ministers.

<u>Kolkhoz</u>

is a collective farm and until recently
the primary form of organization for
agriculture. Theoretically it is a
self-governed cooperative organization
but, in fact, it is controlled from
above. Income for the collective farm
workers is based on shares of income of
the collective farm.

Komsomol

is the Communist youth organization
under the supervision of the Communist
Party. Soviet youth over the age of
sixteen are eligible for membership.

Lengorkom

See <u>Gorkom</u>.

LenNIIP

is the research institute in Leningrad
under the Academy for Construction and
Architecture of the U.S.S.R. Its primary
task is the testing of construction
materials.

Lenobkom

See <u>Obkom</u>.

Lenproekt

is an institute within the Architect-
Planning Department in Leningrad that
drafts original plans and working drawings for most of the buildings constructed by the city.

LenZNIIEP
>is an institute of the Academy for Construction and Architecture in Leningrad that conducts experiments in new types of housing.

LNIIAKKh
>is the Leningrad Institute of the Academy of the Communal Economy for experimenting in the field of capital repairs.

Oblast
>is the major territorial subdivision of the Soviet republics. The Leningrad Oblast, which excludes the city of Leningrad, has a territory of about 84,000 square kilometers.

Obkom (or Lenobkom)
>is the Party committee for the oblast. In the hierarchy of Party organs, it is directly subordinate to the Central Committee of the R.S.F.S.R. In the case of Lenobkom it is superior to the Party Committee of the City of Leningrad (Lengorkom).

Otvetstvenii
>are persons elected from among the occupants of any housing structure with more than three families. They oversee the maintenance of the building and the general behavior of the other tenants. They are responsible to the local housing committees and bureaus.

Presidium of the Lengorsoviet
>is the inner cabinet of the Executive Committee of the City of Leningrad. It is composed of the chairman, first vice-chairmen, other vice-chairmen, and secretary of the Executive Committee.

Prigorod

is the suburban and rural area surrounding an urban center and under city jurisdiction. In Leningrad, five of the rayons (districts) are designated as the prigorod

Rayon (district)

is a territorial subdivision of the oblasts and larger cities. The city of Leningrad is divided in nineteen rayons and the Leningrad Oblast into fifteen primarily rural rayons.

R.S.F.S.R.

is the Russian Soviet Federated Socialist Republic, by far the largest of the fifteen Soviet republics. It stretches from the Baltic Sea to the Pacific Ocean and contains about 55 per cent of the population of the U.S.S.R. Within it lie both Leningrad and Moscow, the latter housing its capital.

Ruble

has been officially set to equal U.S. $0.90, but most observers agree that its true value is somewhat less. The smaller Soviet monetary unit is the kopek; there are 100 kopeks to the ruble.

Soviet

is the council or assembly directly elected by the population at all levels of government. In theory it is the highest organ of government at each level.

Sovkhoz

is a state farm often labelled by the Communists as "a factory in the field." It is usually several thousand acres, and the workers receive a basic salary as in industry.

Sovnarkhozes

were economic regions created by Premier
Nikita Khruschev in 1957 in order to de-
centralize decision-making for the
economy. The U.S.S.R. was divided into
more than 100 such regions with some subsequent changes. They were abolished in
1965 after the fall of Khruschev. The
city of Leningrad and the Leningrad
Oblast formed the Leningrad Sovnarkhoz.

Stroibank

is the state bank for construction. It
supervises financial plans and payments
to trusts and other enterprises engaged
in construction.

Torgov

are the basic retail organizations, each
of which handles a specific category of
retail goods and usually operates several
retail outlets. Some of these organizations are under the direct control of
republic ministries, and others are under
the various local governments.

ZhSK

are housing construction cooperatives
organized among Soviet citizens for the
construction and maintenance of housing
from their private funds for their private use.

Leningrad:
A Case Study
of Soviet Urban
Government

CHAPTER **1** SAINT PETERSBURG--
PETROGRAD--
LENINGRAD

THE FOUNDING OF PETER'S CITY

Leningrad celebrated its 250th anniversary in
June, 1957. By European standards it is a young
city. In 1702 the Russian autocrat, Peter I,
seized the banks of the Neva River flowing into
the shallow Bay of Finland from Sweden. Peter
wanted to confirm to the world his determination
to end Sweden's power over the eastern Baltic region (although his final victory over Sweden did
not come until 1721) and to establish Russia as a
great power to share in Europe's growing hegemony
over the world. It was Russia's first direct sea
route to the West. Peter commanded his serfs to
hack away at the forests of the lowlands, to fill
in the swamps, and to build several permanent
fortresses in order to secure the area and the
coast of the Bay of Finland. Then, as befitting
a great autocrat of the East, he ordered a new
city, Saint Petersburg, to be built in a grand
style on the mouth of the Neva. In 1712, the
capital of all the Russias was moved to Saint
Petersburg. The French architect, Jean Batiste
Leblon, was employed to draw up a general plan for
the city in 1716-17. To fill the grand boulevards,
the Italian architect, Dominico Trezini, and a
succession of other architects and master craftsmen from France, Holland, and Germany were brought
to the new capital to build palaces and government
buildings in the latest styles. Saint Petersburg
quickly became the outstanding example of the
brightly colored baroque cities of eighteenth-century

1

Southern Europe. The new city bore little resem-
blance to the Byzantine-styled character of older
Russian cities with their numerous onion-domed
churches and log buildings. The nobles and intelli-
gentsia who inhabited this new capital also turned
to Western Europe for their education and way of
life and soon came to pride themselves on their
cosmopolitan, Western orientation--a distinction
the city still cherishes.

Although the founding of Saint Petersburg as
a window to the West may have been a successful
political maneuver to establish Russia as a great
power and to enhance the Czar's authority over the
nobility, it began a conflict between Western- and
Slavic-oriented elites that manifested itself in
political rivalry between the traditional capital
of Moscow and the new capital of Saint Petersburg.
This rivalry is still an important factor in the
politics of contemporary Leningrad. Furthermore,
as a physical site for a large city, Peter's choice
leaves something to be desired.[1] The area's marshy
character makes it difficult to build firm founda-
tions and provide adequate drainage. In the fall,
when there is a strong west wind stirring up the
shallow Bay of Finland for several days, the Neva
River rises, and in 1824 and 1924, it seriously
flooded the city. Another hazard has been the damp,
cold climate, aggravated by the swampy character of
the area; this has caused a high incidence of respiratory disease and death in the city, especially
in the crowded slums during the nineteenth and
twentieth centuries. Except for lumber, there are
few natural resources immediately available to the
city. Finally, its very position near the western
frontiers of Russia has made the problem of its
defense formidable.

Nevertheless, Saint Petersburg continued to
grow, and it remained the capital and cultural center of Russia from the time of Peter I through the
Revolutions of 1917. The most significant change
came to the city during the latter part of the
nineteenth century when the capital also became an

important industrial center. The population from
1864 to 1913 increased fourfold. (See Table 1.)
The rapid influx of worker-peasants changed the
character of the city. The new industrial workers
who crowded into the slums of the port district
and the Petrogradskii sections gradually came to
dominate the city and shape the destiny of all the
Russias. They led the revolts against the Czars
in 1905 and early 1917, and against the Provisional
Government in November, 1917. Surprisingly, almost
from the moment of its victory, the city's working
class was abandoned by its leaders, Nikolai Lenin
and Leon Trotsky. Fearing that the position of
the capital was too exposed to anti-Bolshevik and
interventionist forces, Lenin abandoned the cradle
of the Revolution in March, 1918, and moved the capital back to Moscow. The victory of Joseph Stalin
and his anticosmopolitan, anti-international policies confirmed the permanent relocation of the
capital in Moscow. There was no chance of Saint
Petersburg (renamed Petrograd during World War I
to eliminate the supposedly German connotation of
the original name) to retain its former status as
capital. The city had to be content with the honor
of being renamed after Lenin at the time of his
death in 1924, when it became the city of Leningrad.

LENINGRAD UNDER STALIN

The growing shortage of food, the rapid decline of industrial production, and the movement
of the capital to Moscow had left Leningrad de-
pleted and almost a ghost city at the end of the
Civil War. No official figures on the population
were kept, but by extrapolating the census figures
of 1910 and 1926 it is estimated that by 1920 the
number of inhabitants had declined to less than
half that of 1910, and 25 per cent of the living
space was unused.[2]

In the early years of the Soviet regime neither
the central authorities nor local governments were
able to find the means to keep the city's buildings

TABLE 1

Population of Leningrad
(Excluding the suburban areas)

Year	Population
1825	425,000
1864	539,000
1879	1,138,000
1900	1,418,000
1910	1,906,000
1913	2,125,000
1917	2,500,000*
1920	740,000*
1926	1,614,000
1939	3,015,000
1959	2,900,000
1966	3,261,000**

*Estimated figures.

**Including the new territory added to the city proper on January 16, 1963.

Sources: Leningrad i Leningradskaia Oblast v tsifrakh [Leningrad and Leningrad Oblast in Figures] (Leningrad, 1964), p. 13; Narodnoe khoziaistvo R.S.F.S.R. v 1965g [The People's Economy of the R.S.F.S.R. in 1965] (Moscow, 1966), p. 16; Gorodskoe khoziaistvo [The City's Economy] (Leningrad, 1957), pp. 9ff.

in repair, and they rapidly deteriorated. Gas,
which had become the major source of fuel for cooking, was turned off in 1917 and was not again available in the city until 1935. Even during the late
1920's and early 1930's after Stalin had seized
power, the central government took no interest in
restoring Leningrad and provided few funds for
building or expanding economic production. Nevertheless, the local population remained loyal and
independent, and from its own meager resources,
local organs of the Party, city and industry gradually managed to restore the city and preserve it
as an important cultural and industrial center.
Even politically the city refused to give up its
heritage. During the power struggle following
Lenin's death, the Leningrad Party under the leadership of Grigori Zinoviev fought in opposition to
Stalin's takeover of power. As the most proletarian
and revolutionary city, it was only natural that
Leningrad should lead the left opposition to the
"Soviet thermidor." It is not surprising, therefore, that Leningrad's cosmopolitan and independent
attitude angered Stalin, and many Leningraders are
convinced (and Nikita Khrushchev seemed to confirm)
that Stalin was behind the plot in 1934 to assassin-
ate Sergei Kirov, a popular and powerful leader of
the Leningrad Party, and used the assassination as
a pretext for the great purges of the mid-1930's.
These purges were particularly devastating in
Leningrad, where several thousands of both Party
and government leaders were liquidated or removed
to slave-labor camps. Nevertheless, the city remained an important political base and figured in
the post World War II power struggle between
Georgi Zhdanov and Georgi Malenkov and again in
the post-Stalin power struggle in the 1950's. In
the 1940's, the Leningrad Party organization had
come under the control of Zhdanov, and he used it
as a base to extend his authority throughout the
Soviet power structure. After Zhdanov's death,
his appointees were purged or dispersed in what
became known as the notorious Leningrad Affair,
and Malenkov tried to make Leningrad part of his
own power base. Khrushchev, in turn, in his power

struggle against Malenkov, sought to win Leningrad
by filling the city's top Party posts with men who
were likely to support him against Malenkov.

As part of a general policy in the 1930's,
Stalin had tried to emphasize the industrial buildup of central Russia, particularly around the Urals,
and to centralize all control in Moscow. Nevertheless, during the First Five-Year Plans, he had to
abandon the idea of turning Leningrad into a provincial town and was forced to restore it to
an important industrial center. In his frantic
rush for industrial output, Stalin could not ignore
Leningrad, which still had a skilled population
(with 93 per cent literacy) and an important training and industrial base inherited from the Czars.
Furthermore, as a cosmopolitan center, Leningrad
was more attractive to emigrants from the villages
and towns than were the new cities of Siberia.
Initially, the availability of housing must also
have been an important factor. As a result, by
1939, the population had almost doubled to more
than 3 million, and industrial production was
about four and one-half times what it had been in
1913 despite the decline in the 1920's. Leningrad's position as at least the second urban center of Russia seemed assured, until World War II
again threatened to destroy the city.

The fierce loyalty of Leningrad's citizens
was again attested to in the 900-day siege by the
German Army, from August, 1941, to January, 1944.
During this period, the city was almost completely
surrounded by German forces except for a narrow
access route to the east, which in the winter of
1941-42 was confined to a road built on the ice
across Lake Ladoga.[3] The siege extracted a heavy
toll. About one third of the city was destroyed
and about one third of the population was evacuated
or perished, many from starvation.[4] Daily bread
rations were down to as low as 125-200 grams. The
damage was estimated at 4 billion rubles.[5,6] One
fifth or 3.3 million square meters of housing
space was completely destroyed, and another 13

per cent or 2.2 million square meters was significantly damaged. A half million people were without
shelter. At the beginning of the siege, almost
three quarters of the industrial equipment had been
evacuated to safer areas. Industrial production
fell to 32 per cent of 1940, and the number of
workers and employees declined from 1,457,300 to
749,700.

As a result of the fortitude of its people,
Leningrad became the hero city of the Soviet Union
and a symbol of patriotic resistance. But the
siege had again proved Leningrad's extreme vulnerability. As a result, in the postwar reconstruction, Stalin again attempted to shift industrial
production and population centers to the less exposed areas beyond the Urals and tried to restrict
immigration into the cities of European Russia.
Thus again the reconstruction of Leningrad had a
low priority, and it was left to depend largely on
its own devices. The death in 1949 of Zhdanov,
whose power base was the Leningrad Party organization and who had been a leading contender for
Stalin's mantle, further eclipsed Leningrad and
resulted in another major purge of the city's
elite. The postwar cultural purge of intellectuals
and scholars beginning in August, 1946, had already
identified Leningrad as the center of anti-Soviet,
Western influence.

In spite of these obstacles, the recovery of
Leningrad was rapid. With only a small amount of
capital allocated from Moscow, plus a careful mar-
shalling of local resources, 1.6 million square
meters of living space had been restored even before the end of the war, bringing the level of
housing back to 65 per cent of 1940. Complete reconstruction was achieved by 1948, and by 1949 industrial production had reached 128 per cent of
the 1940 level.

In order to hold down the population of Leningrad as well as other large cities, internal pass-
ports were frequently checked, and no one was

allowed to travel to the cities without permission.
Furthermore, no one who did not already possess
housing space in the large cities was permitted to
apply for a job in them. As late as 1958, Khrushche
was calling for a halt to the expansion of the largest cities,[7] but the attraction of the cities as
cultural and entertainment centers could not be resisted. The prohibition on immigration to Moscow
and Leningrad was being systematically ignored
through a variety of ruses. For example, the industrial ministries continued to build an increasing number of factories in both Moscow and Leningrad to take advantage of the already established
supply industries, the community facilities, and
the technical personnel living in the cities. The
expansion of old and new industries in Moscow and
Leningrad in turn required more workers, especially
the semiskilled, who had to be imported. Ministries
also preferred to build in Moscow and Leningrad,
according to Khrushchev, because labor was cheaper.
In order to stay in the big cities, workers were
willing to work for less. Since restrictions had
proved of little value, by about 1959 the de facto
expansion of the population was officially accepted
as inevitable, and major industrial- and home-
building projects were initiated in both Leningrad
and Moscow. Although many of the restrictions on
immigration remained as law, they were rarely enforced. Leningrad's position as the second city
again seemed assured.

ECONOMIC CHARACTERISTICS

Although Leningrad had been founded as a
strategic and capital city, its favorable position
in respect to water transportation and its subsequent development as a rail terminal and an educational center soon brought industry to the area.
At the same time that Peter I ordered the building
of his new capital, he also ordered the construction of a network of canals connecting the city
with central and northern Russia. The first railroads in Russia in the nineteenth century also

emanated from Saint Petersburg. By 1862, the population included 21,000 industrial workers. Toward
the end of the nineteenth century, the government
initiated a major drive for industrialization.
Thus, by 1894, there were 76,000 industrial workers
in Saint Petersburg; by 1902, 133,000 workers; and
by 1913, 242,000 workers. Fine textiles and metal-
lurgical industries, demanding a large number of
skilled workers, were the most prevalent in the
city. In 1902, 33 per cent of Saint Petersburg's
industrial output was in metallurgy and 22.5 per
cent in textiles. Metallurgy is still the most
important industry in Leningrad, with the Kirov
Works being its largest and most famous. Ship-
building (especially naval vessels) and wood and
paper plants were also traditional industries and
continue to play an important role. The first
Soviet atomic commercial vessel was built in Leningrad in 1959. Leningrad has also become noted for
the manufacture of various turbines, diesels, and
electrical equipment. Recently, the Leningrad
chemical industries have been expanded, particularly in the field of plastics. In the area of light
industry, Leningrad specializes in shoes, furniture, woolen and silk textiles, and clothing.
Leningrad produces about one seventh of the output
of light industry in the U.S.S.R. According to
Soviet statistics, the over-all output of industry
is almost twenty times what it was in 1913 and
four times what it was in 1940. The number of industrial workers in greater Leningrad increased
from 242,000 in 1913 to 1,921,546 in 1959. Seventy
per cent of the output is used outside the Leningrad area. Output for some light industries is
shown in Table 2; data are not available for output of other industries in Leningrad, save in per-
centiles of 1958 production.

All industrial production is government owned,
and most of it is controlled from Moscow through
the ministries of the Russian Soviet Federated
Socialist Republic (R.S.F.S.R.), the largest republic of the U.S.S.R., in which Leningrad is
situated. As will be discussed in later chapters,

TABLE 2

Production Figures for Selected Light Industries in Leningrad, Moscow, and the R.S.F.S.R., 1964

Product	Leningrad	Moscow	R.S.F.S.R.
Butters and fats (thousands of metric tons)	19.3	-- *	878.9
Candies (thousands of metric tons)	132.1	278.8	1377.9
Cloth (millions of meters)			
Cotton	222.9	474.5	5924.1
Silk	65.1	338.9	778.2
Wool	13.1	75.3	288.1
Furniture (millions of rubles)	43.0	74.1	987.6
Hosiery (millions of pairs)	80.0	124.5	581.2

Knitted garments (millions of pieces)			
Underwear	25.6	39.3	291.6
Outer garments	10.7	12.0	81.0
Meats (thousands of metric tons)	83.9	127.0	2137.1
Paper (thousands of metric tons)	108.1	6.4	2471.0
Pianos (1963) (thousands)	8.9	-- *	80.6
Prefab housing (millions of square meters)	1.5	3.7	27.6
Refrigerators (thousands)	38.2	208.6	839.4
Shoes (millions of pairs)	39.0	33.2	265.3
Watches and clocks (thousands)	1.85	-- *	25.3

*Information not available.

Source: Narodnoe khoziaistvo R.S.F.S.R. v 1964g [The People's Economy of the R.S.F.S.R. in 1964] (Moscow, 1965).

centralized control of industries has created
serious problems for local officials and undercuts
their authority. In fact, the role of local government in industrial production has declined significantly in recent years. The struggle on the
part of local governments for control of light and
local industry,[8] promised them in the reform of
1957, has been a bitter and losing proposition even
for such a powerful city organization as exists in
Leningrad. In 1958, 14.7 per cent of industrial
production, all concentrated in light industry,
was under the direct control of the Leningrad city
government, but by 1963, only 7.4 per cent still
remained in the hands of the city. In the economy,
the local government's role is currently largely
confined to managing communal services, retail
trade, and housing, but even here--as will be seen--
there are serious conflicts and shortcomings.

Leningrad is also an important transportation
center. Water routes through Lake Ladoga connect
Leningrad by canal and rivers with central and
northern Russia, and from Leningrad railroads fan
north to Archangel, southwest to the Baltic states
and Warsaw, and east and south to Moscow and Kiev.
Within the last few years, an increased network of
truck routes has also begun to emerge around Leningrad, although trucking is still an infant industry
in the Soviet Union.

Supplying the city with foodstuffs is a major
responsibility and concern of the local government
in the U.S.S.R. Because of the persistent shortage
of transportation in the Soviet Union and the low
priority of consumer items, each city had traditionally been forced to depend on the local area
for the bulk of its food. This has been a particular problem for Leningrad, because even though the
territorial boundaries of the city of Leningrad
continue to expand, its territory is largely composed of urban housing and recreational areas. In
1959, only 1 per cent of its population was engaged in agriculture. The major portion of the
agricultural produce, therefore, comes from parts

of Leningrad Oblast (Province) surrounding the city.
Furthermore, the central offices of the oblast are
located in the city, the oblast government is dependent on the city in every other field, and the
two governments (as will be discussed later) are
closely integrated through the Party. Hence the
city is able to coordinate its agricultural needs
with the oblast agricultural departments. (In 1962,
Khrushchev decreed the bifurcation of all Party organizations and local governments into industrial
and agricultural sections, which undermined the integration of local agriculture with the needs of
the city. It was one of the first decrees to be
reversed after he was ousted in 1964.)

Actually, neither the soil nor the climate in
the Leningrad Oblast (Province) is well suited for
agriculture. The growing season is short, and most
of the area is covered by forest, lakes, and low
swamps. Only about 5 per cent of the land is useful for agriculture; most of this is in the south
and primarily suitable for pasture and forage
crops. In 1963, Leningrad Oblast had 225,200 hectares (556,244 acres) of forage crops and 145,500
hectares (359,530 acres) of pasture supporting
303,000 head of cattle, 378,000 pigs, and 103,100
sheep and goats; 58,800 hectares (145,236 acres)
producing 275,000 metric tons of potatoes; 11,200
hectares (27,664 acres) producing 225,000 metric
tons of vegetables; and 56,500 hectares (139,555
acres) producing 62,200 metric tons of grain. Increasingly, the effort to produce grain and vegetables in the area is being abandoned. From 1953
to 1963, the grain acreage had been cut by more
than 60 per cent and vegetables by almost 40 per
cent. With the gradual expansion of truck transportation, it is possible for the first time to
obtain vegetables from the more fertile areas
further south.

Farming in the Leningrad Oblast, as throughout the Soviet Union, is largely organized as collective farms (kolkhozes) or state farms
(sovkhozes). In the Leningrad Oblast the average

size of the collective farm is almost 2,000 hectares (4,942 acres) and the state farm is over
4,000 hectares (9,880 acres).   In 1953, the
kolkhozes farmed two thirds of the 342,100 hectares
(845,329 acres) under cultivation in the Leningrad
Oblast.   By 1963, their share had been reduced to
less than 14 per cent of the 351,800 hectares
(869,298 acres) under cultivation.   The share of
the state farms in the same period went from 22
per cent to 73 per cent.   A small part of the land
under cultivation (22,400 hectares [55,350 acres]
or about 6.5 per cent) is farmed as private plots
by individual collective farmers and workers.   This
is a slight reduction from 1953 when 23,600 hectares (58,316 acres) was under private cultivation.
Although occupying only a small part of the land,
these private producers supplied a significant
amount of the produce.   In the Leningrad Oblast,
for example, they accounted in 1963 for 27 per cent
of the cattle, 25 per cent of the pigs, and 96 per
cent of the sheep and goats; and produced 37 per
cent of the milk, 42 per cent of the meat slaugh-
tered, and 45 per cent of the eggs.

DEMOGRAPHIC CHARACTERISTICS

The 3 million inhabitants of the city of
Leningrad represent only about 1.5 per cent of the
total population of the U.S.S.R., only 3 per cent
of the urban population of the U.S.S.R., and only
3 per cent of the population of the republic
(R.S.F.S.R.).   But because of the wide dispersal
of the population in rural areas and the many towns
and small cities, both Moscow and Leningrad have
played roles far beyond those implied by their size
alone.   It is fair to say that Moscow, Leningrad,
and to a lesser extent Kiev, lead the country politically, culturally, and scientifically.

The 1959 census showed that the population of
Leningrad was almost back to its prewar level and
was growing rapidly at an annual rate of about
610,000. At the time, it was expected that the

city would continue to grow into a large metropoli-
tan area of 5 to 6 million by 1980. But within the
next five years, by 1965, the general decline of
the birth rate in the Soviet Union and the slowing
down of migration to Leningrad had reduced the rate
of increase to 24,000 per year. This trend is con-
tinuing, and the future growth of the city is again
uncertain. (See Tables 3,4, and 13.)

TABLE 3

Birth Rates per Thousand

	Leningrad	Moscow	R.S.F.S.R.
1940	23.6	27.0	33.0
1950	15.5	14.9	26.9
1958	13.0	14.5	24.2
1960	13.4	14.6	23.2
1963	12.0	13.0	18.8
1964	11.9	12.0	16.9

Source: Narodnoe khoziaistvo R.S.F.S.R. v
1965g [The People's Economy of the R.S.F.S.R. in
1965] (Moscow, 1966).

The Leningrad population is quite homogeneous
and is predominantly Great Russian (2.5 million or
88 per cent). By the 1959 census the largest
minority is the Jews (162,000 or 5.6 per cent as
compared to 2 per cent of the Soviet population as
a whole). The remaining minorities are mainly
from European Russia and individually account for
no more than 1 to 2 per cent of the population.
(See Table 5.) As a result of the war, the pre-
dominance of women in the population is even
greater in Leningrad (59 per cent) than for the

TABLE 4

Death Rates per Thousand

	Leningrad	Moscow	R.S.F.S.R
1940	25.6	21.8	20.6
1950	12.1	10.1	10.1
1958	9.3	8.6	7.4
1960	8.9	8.9	7.5
1963	9.2	9.2	7.5
1964	8.6	8.5	7.2

Source: Narodnoe khoziaistvo R.S.F.S.R. v 1965g [The People's Economy of the R.S.F.S.R. in 1965] (Moscow, 1966).

TABLE 5

Population of Leningrad Proper, by Nationality, Based on the 1959 Census

Nationality	Population
Great Russians	2,564,736
Jews	162,344
Ukranians	57,419
White Russians	39,252
Tartars	24,365
Poles	10,751
Estonians	6,717
Armenians	4,540
Latvians	4,188
Lithuanians	2,357
Finns	1,990

Source: Tsentralnoe statistichekoe upravlenie pri Sovete Ministrov S.S.S.R., Itochi vsesoiuznoi perepisi naseleniia 1959g R.S.F.S.R. [The Results of the All-Union Census in 1959, R.S.F.S.R.] (Moscow, 1963), p. 312.

country as a whole (54 per cent). The shortage of
men is particularly acute in the 35 to 50 age
brackets, although not as serious as in the country
as a whole, because the city is able to attract
skilled males in this age category from the rural
areas. Typical of Soviet urban life, the vast
majority of the city's families have less than four
members (89 per cent), and 68 per cent have less
than three. As might be expected, the educational
level in Leningrad is much higher than in the country as a whole, and 7.7 per cent have completed
higher education, compared to 1.8 per cent for the
national average. Another 22 per cent have finished
their middle-school education, compared to 9 per
cent of the U.S.S.R. As a center of education, research, and technology, it is also not surprising
that over 40 per cent of Leningrad's working population is classified as employee and professional,
as compared to 20 per cent for the country as a
whole. Most of the others are classified as workers.

Typical of Soviet Russia, a high percentage
(almost 60 per cent) of the city's population is
employed. Children under sixteen make up about 20
per cent of the population, and another 5.5 per
cent are on pensions. The high number of employed
persons is due not only to the small number of
older people (less than 9 per cent of the population is sixty years and older), but also to the
fact that a large proportion of older people are
forced to work because they have either no other
income or must augment their meager pensions.
Furthermore, 75 per cent of the women between the
ages of sixteen and fifty-four work. Most families
find it difficult to live on only the salary of the
father.

THE CITY AND ITS REGION

Leningrad, as mentioned previously, was
founded on the delta of the Neva River, flowing
into the Bay of Finland. The city and the immediate surrounding area form the Karelian Isthmus,

between the Bay of Finland and the large inland
lake, Lake Lodoga. The lake is situated about 30
kilometers (19 miles) east and northeast of Leningrad and is the source of the Neva River. As the
window to the West, the city immediately became an
important port and naval base even though the bay
and the city are icebound during the winter months.
The naval base itself (and home port of the Soviet
Baltic Fleet) is located on the small Island of
Kronshtadt (12 square kilometers--4.6 square miles)
about 40 kilometers (25 miles) from Leningrad, but
it is administered as part of the city.

Until World War II, the Finnish boundary was
only a few miles north of Leningrad. It was largely a desire to remedy this vulnerability that
prompted Stalin to initiate the war with Finland
in 1939 and push the border back 150 kilometers
(93 miles) from Leningrad. Except for the city of
Viborg, the Karelian Isthmus seized from Finland
is composed of forests, lakes, and farms.

Unlike most Western cities of this size,
Leningrad is not surrounded by densely populated
suburban areas. In fact, as with most Soviet
cities, there is no transitional zone between city
and country. The outermost groups of apartment
buildings are right next to collective farms or
forests. Even though it lacks large suburban areas
Leningrad exercises much more control over the area
surrounding it than do most cities in the West.
Leningrad has under its direct jurisdiction not
only the fourteen urban districts or rayons covering an area of slightly more than 500 square kilometers (190 square miles) which is called the city
proper, but also an additional five rural or suburban rayons composed of almost 700 square kilometers (270 square miles). This makes it possible
for the Leningrad Soviet to integrate the economies
of the immediately surrounding towns and to plan
expansion of the city and the greenbelt recreational area circling the city. Furthermore, the
borders of the city have been expanded from time
to time; the last major change was January 16, 1963

when both the city proper and its suburban area
(prigorod) were enlarged.

The jurisdictions within and around Leningrad
are thus several: (1) nineteen districts or rayons
within the city of Leningrad; (2) the so-called
city proper, consisting of the fourteen rayons
that are urban; (3) the five rural or suburban rayons of the city within which there are about twenty-
five towns and workers' settlements; and (4) the
Leningrad province or oblast, encompassing a large
agricultural region around the city but exclusive of it.

In the suburban area under the city's jurisdiction live about 400,000 people and in the Leningrad Oblast (Province), which covers an additional
area of 84,000 square kilometers (32,432 square
miles) surrounding the city, live another 1,328,400,
of which 43 per cent are farmers. Within 43 miles
of the city center, there are thirty-nine satellite
towns, including those within the city's jurisdiction, with a total population of about 750,000
people, but none has over 50,000, and most have
20,000 inhabitants or less.[9] The majority of the
satellite towns are located in the south and grew
up around the summer palaces of the Czar and the
nobility. The main exceptions are Kolpino and
Sestroretsk, which developed around munitions factories. Even before the Revolution, some of the
towns developed industries feeding into Saint
Petersburg, but by comparison with the city they
were of minor importance. Under the Soviet regime,
as part of the general plan to disperse industries
(a goal from the 1930's that has never been applied in practice), industrial output in the
satellite towns did expand somewhat, but by and
large they remain primarily market towns, sana-
toriums and recreation centers, branch centers
for scientific institutions in Leningrad, and suburban communities. From the satellite towns about
140,000 commuters come daily, but they represent
less than 10 per cent of the working force of the
city. Three fourths of the commuters come by
train over the following lines: Moscow Line, 30

per cent; Karelian Line, 28 per cent; Baltic Line,
27 per cent; Eastern Line to Petrokrepost, 6 per
cent; Warsaw Line, 5 per cent; and the Eastern Line
to Volkhov, 4 per cent.[10]

CONCLUSION

City planners from the West may look with envy
at the development of the city of Leningrad because
it has escaped to date some of the major problems
plaguing most of the large metropolises of the rest
of the world. There are no large sprawling suburbs
and satellite cities to turn the center of the city
into a run-down ghetto. The population is neither
a polyglot of very rich and very poor nor a seeth-
ing conglomerate of minorities difficult to integrate into the general population. Leningrad has
even been able to hold down the influx of the rural
population and currently the population seems to be
stabilizing. Finally, the traditional austerity of
the Soviet system has allowed the city to avoid being overwhelmed by material goods and private trans
portation. Thus, ideally, the city can face the
pending but gradual increase of affluence with the
lessons of Western cities before it and planning
made possible by a strong centralized system of
government.

But can Leningrad, in fact, in the next couple
of decades fulfill the promise of its propaganda
and become a model of the best in city planning?
In the past it has shown the spirit necessary to
resist becoming just another provincial city or
the decayed ruins of an imperial past destroyed by
the centralizing tendencies of Moscow. Is this
spirit still strong? Does the city have the organization and the means to plan meaningfully and
successfully for the future? The next chapters
will investigate the operations and structure of
the city's government, its ability to cope with
the current problems, and the plans that are being
made for its future.

NOTES TO CHAPTER 1

1. There are many similarities between the
founding of Washington, D.C. and Saint Petersburg.
Both cities were constructed on low swampy lands
that had not yet been developed, in order for the
new capitals to be free of pressures from older developed regions and to break with the past. The
founding of both cities was an attempt to turn the
country to new directions. Washington, D.C. became
the symbol of a new strong union of the former
British colonies and weak confederation, and Saint
Petersburg became the head of a new Russia dedi-
cated to modernization and a strong central government oriented toward Western Europe. In both cases,
foreign architects were hired to plan for the
future development of the city on a grand scale,
and each soon outgrew these plans with the rapid
expansion of the scope of government and the population of the city.

2. S. I. Lomov and N. N. Petrov, in an article in Gorodskoe khoziaistvo [The City's Economy]
(Leningrad, 1957), p. 9, estimated the population
of Leningrad to be 740,000 in 1920.

3. For a detailed discussion, see Leon Goure,
The Siege of Leningrad (Stanford, 1962).

4. See Gorodskoe khoziaistvo [The City's
Economy], pp. 17-19. Some estimated the population to have reached a low point of less than 1
million in 1942; see A. V. Karasev, Leningradtsi
v godi blokadi, 1941-1943 [The People of Leningrad
in the Years of Blockade, 1941-1943] (Moscow, 1959),
pp. 185, 254-57.

5. N. Manakov and N. Petrov, Gorodskoe
khoziaistvo Leningrada [The Economy of the City of
Leningrad] (Leningrad, 1949), pp. 129-30.

6. All values in rubles used in this study
are as much as possible converted to current rubles.
The official rate of exchange is one ruble equals
U.S. $0.90.

7.   Pravda, March 15, 1958.

8.   Local industry is the term applied to those enterprises making products primarily for local consumption.

9.   Gorodna--sputniki (Sbornik statei) [Satellite Towns: A Collection of Articles] (Moscow, 1961), pp. 50-51.

10.   Ibid., p. 57.

CHAPTER **2** THE POLITICAL
STRUCTURE

THE GENERAL CHARACTER OF
SOVIET LOCAL GOVERNMENT

Although Leningrad--as Russia's second city
and cosmopolitan center--is unique in some ways,
the general pattern of its local politics is similar to that of other Soviet cities, except Moscow.
In analyzing the government of Leningrad it is,
therefore, necessary to describe some of the general features of Soviet local government. The most
important characteristic is the subordination of
local government to the central authorities. Under
the Constitution, the U.S.S.R. has a federal structure with authority divided between the All-Union
Government and the republics. This is in part reflected in the allocations of various matters to
several types of ministries. Matters considered
to be of strictly national concern are under the
authority of All-Union ministries. Issues to be
dealt with concurrently, for which the All-Union
Government sets the basic policies and the republic governments define and carry out these policies, are organized around union-republic ministries. Matters of only regional concern are
directly under the ministries of the individual
republics. However, even in the last instance,
the All-Union Government in practice assumes over-
all supervision.

Questions relating to local government are
handled by union-republic ministries or republic
ministries. Both urban and rural local governments

are wards of the republics and derive their authority from the republics. Leningrad is under the
government of the R.S.F.S.R., the largest Soviet
republic, stretching from the Baltic Sea to the
Pacific Ocean. The capital of the R.S.F.S.R. is
Moscow, which is also the capital of the Soviet
Union as a whole. Because Moscow houses both the
ministries of the R.S.F.S.R. and those of the
U.S.S.R., and because the R.S.F.S.R. is by far the
most important republic, the policies of these two
levels of government are closely intertwined.

The federal structure of the Soviet Union has
not been stable, and particularly from Stalin's
death in 1953 changes in the distribution of functions and responsibilities have been frequent. Up
through the 1950's, the basic legislation controlling local government came from statutes passed
either by the All-Union Government or by republic
A governments. ⌜As part of a decentralization and
rationalization process, in August, 1957, the All-
Union Government passed a decree invalidating all
statutes of the U.S.S.R. that dealt with local government, thus leaving it up to each republic to
draft comprehensive statutes on rural and urban
local government. Most republics have complied,
but the all-important Russian Republic (R.S.F.S.R.)
had yet to draft a statute for urban government as
of the writing of this text. Thus, the city of
Leningrad continues to function on the basis of old
invalidated statutes, but in the Soviet context
this does not in fact greatly hinder the operation
of local government. The only concern is that a
new statute might significantly alter the system.
It is at least probable that some of the cautious
experimentation in local administration now taking
place in Leningrad and other Soviet cities will be
B reflected in the new statute.⌟ Although at the
time of the decentralization reform, an expansion
of the authority of local government was contem-
plated, in practice, as will be seen, no such expansion has taken place to date. However, a partial rationalization of operations has resulted,
by means of gradually concentrating authority for

the city services in one jurisdiction rather than
spreading it among several.

Although currently all directives to the city
come directly from the R.S.F.S.R. government--
issued either by a specific ministry or by the
R.S.F.S.R. Council of Ministers--the origins or
initiatives for the directives are more often than
not the All-Union Government or a higher Party organ. However, it is usually not possible specifically to discover where a directive originates,
and for the purpose of this study it is not very
important. As a matter of convenience, therefore,
we have designated all directives originating in
Moscow, whether formally coming from the Party,
All-Union, or republic organs as coming from so-
called central or higher authorities.

In contrast to the West, where city charters A
tend to establish a stable, almost permanent allocation of functions and authority to a city government, allocation in the Soviet Union is forever
changing. The powers of the city government of
Leningrad, the city's boundaries, and its personnel
can be and have been frequently changed by the All-
Union and Russian Republic authorities, with or
without reference to local interests. For example,
the boundaries of Leningrad and its rayons recently
were changed twice by the R.S.F.S.R. Council of
Ministries, once on January 16, 1963, and again on
January 11, 1965.

The second and most important feature of   B
Soviet local government is the role of the Communist
Party as the focus of power and coordinator within
the city, and between the city and other levels of
governments. The administrative organization of
the Party parallels that of the local government
but is distinct from it. As will be discussed in
a later section, it can apply its control and discipline to government administrators at all levels.

A third distinction of Soviet local adminis-   C
tration is that city governments are responsible

not only for the public services traditionally provided in Western municipalities by local government, but they are also responsible for supplying,
or at least coordinating, supply of all the daily
economic and social needs of their citizens. The
general policies and many of the specific directives under which city governments manage these
services, however, are handed down to the local
authorities by the republic's council of ministers
or its ministries.

The fourth general characteristic of the Soviet
system is the fact that in priority for allocation
of tax proceeds and material resources, local governments are near the bottom and traditionally have
operated on a bare minimum. Furthermore, they have
few revenue sources of their own.

Another feature of Soviet local administration
is the role played by the citizenry. Although
large numbers of citizens are elected to the several local soviets and various public committees
in the city, they have little or no part in or influence on local politics or administration, which
is the exclusive domain of the professional Party
administrators and local government administrators
under direction from Moscow.

In sum, because the policy-making function of
local authorities is severely restricted, the local
executive committees of the Party and government
serve as preliminary planning organs and coordinating agencies for the field representatives of the
central government's ministries and departments
that provide daily necessities and services to the
population. Only in very limited areas do the
local committees have the power to initiate and
carry out programs without reference to central
authorities.

The city of Leningrad follows the general pattern of Soviet local government. Nevertheless, it
has certain advantages over most cities in the
Soviet Union. Because of its size, it is subordinate directly to the R.S.F.S.R. Council of

Ministers and is not subordinate to an <u>oblast</u> (provincial) government. ⎡In fact, it has a position   A
superior to that of an <u>oblast</u> government, because
it contains a population with a significant number
of the country's Party and intellectual elite and,
therefore, carries great political weight in Moscow.
Furthermore, its long tradition of autonomy has
given it more jurisdiction over such important
areas as housing and retail trade than all other
cities in the U.S.S.R., including Moscow.⎦

COORDINATING EXECUTIVE BODIES

In theory, the highest governmental authority
and legislative body of Leningrad is the city
soviet, made up of over 600 elected representatives (about one deputy for every 6,000 inhabitants). Elections for the city soviet and other
local soviets are held every two years. In theory,
deputies can be nominated by the Party, youth organizations, trade unions, or any mass organization
or group of activists. In fact, the nominating
process is in charge of the Party, but the Party
is constantly exhorted to consult widely with mass
groups to find popular and qualified representatives. There is only one nominee for each post,
and he wins normally with the support of 99 per
cent of the electorate. Only in unusual circum-
stances have nominees for local soviets in some
localities failed to obtain 50 per cent of the
vote, but there is no evidence that this has occurred in Leningrad since World War II. Election
as a deputy is looked upon as an honor by the
Party, which tends to nominate people who are prom-
inent in various professions. From the evidence
that is available, it appears that the average
citizen also looks upon nomination as an honor,
and he accords the deputy due respect.

Once elected, the city soviet is called into
session by its executive committee or presidium,
three or four times a year. Each of its meetings
lasts one day or a part of the day. Except as a

symbol of legitimacy and Soviet-type democracy, the
city soviet in no way controls the city government.
An indication of the duties and importance of the
deputy in local administration is that one general
room is set aside for the use of the 600 deputies
and that no desks or other meeting rooms are available to them in the city hall. The real purpose
of the soviet is to serve as a propaganda instrument by approving those decrees to which the local
authorities want to give special weight. It also
performs a legitimizing function by approving the
yearly budget and plan and by unanimously electing
its executive committee and presidium, which actually run the city government and the city court.
The city court is composed of a chairman, 3 vice-
chairmen, and 45 members. There are also 506 lay
assessors. Lay assessors are elected from the educated citizenship. Two lay assessors and one professional judge, as a panel, serve as judge and
jury in soviet trials. The only operating function
of the city soviet and other local soviets is organizing mass participation. (See the section in
this chapter on "Mass Participation in Local Government" for additional information.)

Although the city soviet as a whole wields
little power, the individual deputy is an important cog in the political wheel, acting as a vital
link between the citizen and his local government.
This constituent-deputy relationship provides an
important safety valve in a highly regulated and
controlled system. Deputies are required to hold
office hours for their constituents at least once
a week. In practice, many citizens use this opportunity to petition the government. They do not
come, however, to demand action, as is so often
the case in Western countries; rather, they come
as suppliants humbly petitioning the deputy to in-
tercede on their behalf to overcome red tape or an
arbitrary action. Most come after some hesitation
and only when their situation becomes desperate
and requires intercession. There is a reluctance
on the part of most citizens to become involved in
disputes with the authorities. Primarily, constituents approach their deputy about pensions,

alleged unfairness with respect to dismissal from
jobs, inadequate housing, or unfair treatment by
housing officials. The deputy is supposed to investigate each complaint thoroughly. Quite often
the deputy is able to straighten the matter out to
the benefit of his constituent. In fact, the central authorities often complain about the leniency
of both local officials and the courts on these
human issues when pressed by a deputy.

As part of the campaign in recent years to revitalize the local soviets and to enhance the
deputy's position, the central government began
publishing the monthly journal, Soveti Deputatov
Trudiashchikhsia (Deputies of the Working People),
in 1957. The magazine's main emphasis is given to
the proper relations of the deputy with the masses.

During debate on the transition to popular
rule under Communism, there has been some discussion in the press that advocates giving the individual deputy some genuine authority, such as the
right to require local officials to cease engaging
in unauthorized or illegal practices.[1] But as yet
no real authority in either theory or practice has
been granted to deputies at any level.

The Executive Committee of the city soviet in
Leningrad is composed of from twenty-three to
twenty-five members. Although there are no formal
requirements that the Executive Committee and the
heads of the leading departments be elected deputies of the city soviet, this is the usual practice.
Chart 1 shows a typically composed Executive Committee. Less than a third of the city government's
more than thirty departments are directly represented on the Leningrad Executive Committee. Those
included are considered to be the most important,
and the inclusion of their Chiefs on the Executive
Committee is more or less constant. It should be
noted from Chart 1 that only one member of the
Executive Committee is designated as a worker, pre-
sumably to give the Committee the working-class
character of which Soviet propaganda boasts.

CHART 1

Typical Composition of an Executive
Committee of a City Soviet

Chairman

Secretary

Two First Vice-Chairmen

Four Vice-Chairmen (One of Whom Also Heads the
City's Planning Commission)

Chairman of One Urban Rayon in the City

The First Secretary of the City Party Committee

One First Secretary of One Urban Rayon Party
Committee

One Factory Director

One Worker

Eleven Chiefs of the Leading Departments of City
Government
 Architects and Planning
 Construction of Housing, Public Buildings, and
   Industry
 Daily and Personal Services
 Education
 Finance
 Housing
 Industrial Construction Materials
 Local Industry
 Local Trade
 Security
 Welfare

The actual mode of appointment to the Executive Committee is obscure. It is known that the
city's Party committee (gorkom) and its subcommittee on appointments (nomenklatura) play a leading
role. But beyond designating the chairman of the
Executive Committee, it is not known whether the
Party committee initiates other appointments or
merely exercises a veto. Several members, such as
the department heads of architect-planning, security, finance, and education, are appointed by their
respective central and republic ministries and
hold their positions on the Executive Committee as
representatives of these important ministries.
The fact that the Party has at times specifically
dismissed members of the Executive Committee would
seem to indicate that the Party secretary exercises
close control over the personnel of the city government.

In one sense, having the appointments made or
closely controlled by the Party makes them strictly
political, but because differences in political
attitudes are not permitted, and Soviet personnel
at all levels consciously avoid developing any individual political views and accept the Party line
unquestioningly, the criterion for appointment is
not political loyalty to one view or another. A
man is chosen rather for his skills. This criterion is confirmed by the fact that success in
fulfilling economic plans and directives appears
to be the primary basis for promotion of both Party
and government personnel; thus, the appointment of
a skilled, experienced administrator is vital to a
Party secretary's own advancement. There is, however, one important exception to this pattern. In
the struggle for power within the Party, the various top contenders seek the appointment to crucial
offices of men who are personally loyal to themselves. But it is impossible to know how far down
in the hierarchy personal loyalty may be a factor
in recruitment. The widespread purges in the Leningrad city government after Zhdanov's death suggest
that appointments based on personal loyalty or be-
lieved personal loyalty to Zhdanov had been quite

widespread.   It is doubtful, however, that such far
reaching personal empires are the general rule today, even in Leningrad.   If such a personal empire
is risky for a member of the Politburo, it is un-
likely that an oblast or city Party secretary would
dare engage widely in such independent activities.
Furthermore, his tenure in office in any one place
is usually not long enough, as transfers are frequent.

Executive Committee meetings are held every
two weeks and tend to be rather perfunctory, merely
approving the actions and regulations of the chairman and the Presidium.   As one of the two largest
cities in the U.S.S.R., Leningrad was recently
given the legal right to organize a Presidium of
the Executive Committee.   Informally the Presidium
has existed for many years.   It is composed of the
chairman, secretary, the first vice-chairmen and
vice-chairmen of the Executive Committee.   This
body meets frequently--two or three times a week--
and has become increasingly the center of the city
government.   The Chairman and the Secretary of the
Executive Committee also have the legal right to
issue orders on their own, as long as these are
subsequently approved by the Executive Committee.
Soviet legal writers try to make a great deal of
the difference between orders issued by the Chairman and regulations passed by the Executive Committee, but the distinction is purely semantic.   Sub-
stantively they differ neither as to content nor
as to authority.   In effect, the Chairman of the
Executive Committee is the chief executive officer,
although Soviet legal writings disclaim that the
chairman has any special or superior status or
powers of his own.   The actual power the chairman
chooses to exercise also seems to vary considerably
with the holder of the office.   V. Ia. Isaev, who
came into office in 1963, has expanded the importance of the office considerably and acts almost
like a powerful mayor of an American city.[2]

As the highest governmental authority and coordinating body of Leningrad, the Presidium has

arrayed around itself the various branches of government. Each of its officers is made responsible
for a group of departments and other offices. (See
Chart 2.) Through this mechanism, the city government achieves what appears to be a high degree of
centralization of its complete structure.

The resolutions passed by the Presidium and   A
Executive Committee appear to serve at least five
discernible functions:

1. In certain areas such as housing, trade,
and parks they determine with the force of law the
city government's broadest operational and budget
policies (within the directives laid down by the
higher organs of government).

2. They establish public regulations for the
use of various services such as the public baths,
trolley buses, and barber shops.

3. They are often used to administer in detail certain departmental matters. For example,
each fall an order is passed concerning snow removal, specifying the priority of streets to be
cleared and the methods of snow removal to be used.
These priorities change from year to year.

4. In conjunction with trade unions they organize socialist competitions and honor rolls for
departments and enterprises that overfulfill their
plans.

5. Resolutions of the Executive Committee are
also frequently used to discipline subordinates.
It is typical of Soviet administrative practice to
discipline both organs and personnel by means of
public criticism. About 25 per cent of the published resolutions are of this type, denouncing
the shortcomings of the various departments and
specifically ordering the chiefs of those departments to remedy the situation. There seems to be
no attempt to differentiate between departments
directly subordinate to the Executive Committee

CHART 2

Presidium Executive Committee Officials and Agencies
Supervised and Coordinated by Them

Chairman of the Executive Committee

Department of Cadres and Instruction*
Statistical Department*
Finance Department*
Management of Internal Affairs*
Management of Fire Safety
Gorvoenkomat (Civil Defense
   Organization)

First Vice-Chairman

Department of Education*
Culture Management*
Management of Movies
Management for the press*
Committee for Radio and Television*
Soiuzpechat (Council of the Press)

First Vice-Chairman

Chief management of Automobile Transport
Fuel and Energy management*
Management of the city telephone system
Management of Garden-Park Economy and
   Forest Construction*
Management of Gas Supplies*
Management of Roads and Bridges*
Management of the subway
Management of Water and Sewage*
Tram-Trolleybus management*
Lenmetrostroi (Trust for Construction of
   the Subway)
Institute Leniproinzhproekt (Architectural
   Planning)
Society for the Preservation of Nature
City Staff for the Welfare of Leningrad

Vice-Chairman

Chief Management for Civil Construction*
Chief of management of Construction
   Materials*
Architect-Planning management*
Management of Capital Construction*
Committee on the Question of New Construc-

Vice-Chairman*

Housing management*
Capital Repair management*
Management of Costs and Allocation of Housing Space*

Vice-Chairman

Planning commission*
Management of Day-to-Day Services*
Management of communal service enterprises
Supply management*
Technical management*
Trust Leningradodezhda (Clothing Trust)
Arbitration Tribunals
City Bureau of Technical Inventory

Vice-Chairman

Chief management of general provisions*
Chief management of trade*
City drug management
Management of bread industries*
Department of Veterinary
Department of Welfare*
Summer season trust
Committee on physical culture and sports

Secretary

Archives Department*
Department of Internal Relations*
Department of Social Security*
General Department*
Organization-Instruction Department*
Registry Department
Juridical Section
Legal Profession Organization
City Courts
General Inspection of the Controller
Reception Committee of Executive Committee
Committee on Questions of Religious Culture

*Departments formally listed as directly subordinate to the Executive Committee of the City Soviet.

Source: Biulleten ispolkoma Lengorsoveta [Bulletin of the Executive Committee of the Leningrad City Soviet], No. 9, 1965.

and those responsible both to the Executive Committee and a republic ministry. Both are freely criti
cized in the resolutions.

A   Perhaps even more revealing are the areas in
which the Executive Committee passes none or very
few resolutions. These include all matters of educational policy, police powers and regulations,
fire and safety regulations, methods of financial
control, tax and revenue regulations (except arrangements for the selling of lottery tickets),
and public welfare. Only 10 per cent of the Committee's resolutions are in these areas, and most
of them merely implement resolutions that have already been passed by the Council of Ministers of
the R.S.F.S.R.

It is clear that the Executive Committee and
its Presidium do not function as policy-making
bodies in the tradition of a city council. As
will be seen in areas such as housing construction,
however, they have the power to initiate or suggest
certain plans, but these must then be approved by
higher authorities. Even its role as an executive
body is only partial. In the important areas of
police, taxes, education, public safety, and welfare they do not have even the power to issue minor
regulations. Only in such matters as housing, some
areas of retail trade, restaurant operation, parks,
transportation, and culture do they act as the
executive authority.

B   As its organizational chart suggests, the
Executive Committee is looked upon as a local coordinating body. Through the Committee and its
subdivisions, the various local offices of national
republic, and regional ministries and departments
providing the daily needs of the population are coordinated with each other and with the few departments under exclusive local jurisdiction. Omitted
from the coordinating function of the Executive
Committee are the regional offices in Leningrad of
union-republic and All-Union ministries, the operations of major industries, long-distance transportation, the various research institutes, and the

schools of higher learning in Leningrad. The city
government, however, does have some control and
contact with these organizations, particularly in
respect to the construction of new buildings and
supply of services. (See Chapters 4 and 5.) Furthermore, in some Soviet cities other than Leningrad, the major portions of retail trade and housing are also excluded from local coordination.
Liaison with these organizations is accomplished in
part through the integration of the Communist Party
and trade unions into the system of local govern-
ment. | This will be discussed in detail in the fol-
lowing section of this chapter.

⌐ In the years of 1957-64, when the national   A
economy was organized into economic regions
(sovnarkhozes), the coordination of local government with national institutions situated in Leningrad was made easier. The vice-chairman of the
local economic region (sovnarkhoz) was included on
the Executive Committee, and the chairman of the
city's Presidium served on the Executive Committee
of the economic region. But apparently the resulting cooperation was too close, and the sovnarkhoz
was accused of localism and favoring the city over
national interests. With the removal of Khrushchev,
the economic regions, and with them local integra-
tion of the economy, were abolished. |

⌐ Traditionally the task of coordination at the ß
local level has been the responsibility of the
Presidium, the Department of Internal Relations,
and the Organization-Instruction Department. Recently the means of coordination have been supple-
mented by the appointment of high-level coordinating subcommittees designed to deal with such specific problems as housing and juvenile delinquency.
These subcommittees are composed not only of the
chiefs of interested bureaus and departments--in-
cluding those subordinate to republic ministries
in Moscow--but specially qualified outside members
who may be appointed as well. In addition, there
is always a leading representative from the local
Party organization and from the oblast trade-union

council on the subcommittee. Representatives from
national research and higher educational institutions in Leningrad often are also included. Some
of the more important of these include committees
on: Communal Services in New Areas, Public Services, Department Archives, Management of Housing,
Capital Repairs, Naming of Streets and Parks,[3]
Youth Affairs, Materials for Industry and Construction, and Construction. One purpose of these committees is to coordinate activities on such crucial
problems as the perennial shortage of materials and
supplies. In addition, by their bringing in top
leaders from organs outside the executive committee
responsibility for fulfillment of plans is shared
with other organs, and the prestige of these leaders can be used to get a better hearing in Moscow.

THE LENINGRAD PARTY ORGANIZATION

Parallel to the governmental structure, the
Party maintains territorial organizations at the
rayon, city, and oblast level. The major difference is that the Party organization of the city is
subordinate rather than equal to the Party organization of the province. Like the soviets, the
highest authority at each level is in theory the
Party conference, made up of representatives electe
from the next lower level. Because it meets once
every two years, authority is exercised in the interim by the committees elected by the conferences.
The conference also elects a revision commission
and the director of the Party newspaper. The
Leningrad Oblast Committee (Lenobkom) has 98 members and 47 candidate members; the Leningrad City
Committee (Lengorkom) has 87 members and 35 candidates. Candidate members may attend and participate in discussions at the meetings but may not
vote. Candidacy is usually a stepping stone to
full membership. These committees, while important, meet only occasionally, and the real policy-
making bodies of the Party are the bureaus. There
are 13 members and 2 candidate members on the
oblast bureau; there are 11 members and 2 candidate

members on Leningrad's city bureau. The administration of the Party and, in fact, the real leaders at
the local level are the secretaries, and they hold
full-time positions. At the oblast level, the
Party boss is the first-secretary, assisted by a
second-secretary and three additional secretaries.
At the city level, there is also a first-secretary,
a second-secretary, and three secretaries, but at
the rayon level there are only a first-secretary
and two secretaries. In addition to the secretaries
at the oblast, city, and rayon levels, there are
about 4,500 paid Party personnel in Leningrad, including the secretaries of the primary organizations and other functionaries. Primary organizations are the basic units of the Party, formed in
industrial enterprises, state and collective farms,
and governmental, educational, cultural, scientific,
and trading institutions, and, in exceptional cases,
mainly rural, in residential areas.

In 1940, Leningrad had about 220,000 Party
members, and in 1952 the membership had risen to
222,615. By 1961, it had increased to 292,000 members, and by 1964, to 330,000 members. This represents about 10 per cent of the population or about
15 per cent of the adult citizens over the age of
twenty-five. Of the 330,000 Communists in Leningrad, there are: 100,000 workers; 77,000 engineers
and technicians; 35,000 participants in science,
education, culture, medicine, and arts (of which
15,000 are students, 4,000 are physicians, and
4,500 are in literature and arts). More than half
the members have higher or middle education, and
6,140 have doctors' degrees or are scientific candidates. To this must be added about 500,000 members of the Komsomols, the Party organization for
youths between fifteen and twenty-six years of age.
There were 6,221 primary Party organizations in
the city and oblast in 1964.[4]

One of the pertinent features of the professional Party hierarchy throughout the Soviet Union,
at least at the lower levels, has been the stress
on turnover. The desirability of such turnover

was repeatedly stressed by Khrushchev and embodied
in Party statutes. Since the removal of Khrushchev
there has been evidence of the increasing stability
of Party officeholders, particularly at higher
levels and of resistance to the influx of younger
members.[5] In 1963, however, there was a 70 per
cent turnover among secretaries of primary organizations in Leningrad; in the elections of Party
committees in 1963-64, 60 per cent of the membership of the new committees had never been elected
before. Party secretaries are in theory elected by
the membership or conference but in fact are appointed from above, and frequent transfers and pro-
motions of secretaries are part of a planned proces
to train personnel, find new leadership, advance
younger Party members, and prevent "localism."

THE ROLE OF THE PARTY
IN LOCAL GOVERNMENT

An important part of the coordinating role of
the city government is played by the Communist
Party. In fact, the Party and government are so
intermingled at local levels as well as higher
levels that often it is not discernible who plays
what role. All members of the city's Executive
Committee are members of the Party, and, therefore,
they are subject to its discipline. But more important, top members of the Party apparatus are
members of the Executive Committee, and leading
members of the Executive Committee are on the city
and provincial Party committees. V. Ia. Isaev,
Chairman of the Executive Committee for the city,
is a member of both Party committees as well as
the Party executive bureaus of both the city and
province. G. I. Popov, First-Secretary of the
city Party organization, is a member of the city's
Executive Committee. In addition, ten members of
the Executive Committee in 1965 were also members
of the city Party committee, and two were members
of the provincial committee. (Four members of the
Executive Committee were also delegates to the
Twenty-Third Party Congress in 1966.) One rayon

Party secretary is also included, as a rule, on the Executive Committee.

It is Isaev's membership in the oblast Party organs that provides the primary means of coordinating the city and oblast governments. At the same time, the city Party organization works closely with the oblast Party structure, and about thirty Party leaders hold positions on the committee and executive bureaus of both. Thus, the top leaders of the Party and government in the city and province form an inner elite and jointly control local politics.

On its own, the city government has few formal contacts with industries of republic and All-Union subordination, the research institutes, and institutions of higher learning in Leningrad. The Party performs the liaison role with these. Because of the regime's particular concern with industrial development, the Party expends most of its efforts in this area. In Leningrad, the Party has been especially successful in maintaining its influence and control over industry, because some 47 per cent of the industrial workers are Party members and 64 per cent of the local secretaries have engineering and technical degrees. But with the educational and technical institutes, the Leningrad Party organs have been less successful. The chief contacts and support for these institutions are in Moscow and in the powerful Academy of Sciences in Moscow and Leningrad. Their leaders are the indispensable, high status scientific elite who very often shun politics. Only 11.2 per cent of their personnel are members of the Party, and their primary organs usually report directly to Party agencies in Moscow.

The rules and program of the Communist Party provide that the Party organs at all levels should issue the leading directives to governmental bodies. The Party organs are the acknowledged policy-making centers of the system rather than the various committees of government. In Leningrad, the most

important resolutions of the city's Executive Committee are signed by both the chairman of the Execu
tive Committee and the first-secretary of the city'
Party committee. But a close examination of these
resolutions and of others that lay down basic
changes and policies indicates that in almost all
cases they are merely implementing resolutions of
decrees passed earlier by the R.S.F.S.R. Council of
Ministers and higher Party organs.

A   It has been a common notion in the West that
under Khrushchev policy-making became more decentralized. At the republic level and for a time in
industry, this seems to have held true. For all
republics except the Russian Republic (R.S.F.S.R.),
the decentralization decrees have resulted in a
significant increase in authority. For the Russian
Republic, which contains over half the population
and the major portion of the land area of the
U.S.S.R., actual decentralization is not so evident
because the All-Union Government and the Russian
Republic (R.S.F.S.R.) Government in Moscow work
closely together and are organizationally integrated. This is also true of the All-Union and
B R.S.F.S.R. Party organs. At the level of local
government, the trend of authority was actually in
the opposite direction, toward greater centralization. Under Stalin, there was extreme centralization of the basic economy, and in order to insure
the tight and close control which Stalin demanded,
administrators found it necessary to give their
primary attention to a few key indices, mostly in
heavy industry. Questions concerning administration of local government and most of the consumer-
goods industry which it partially controlled were
not generally included in the category of essen-
tials. Therefore, over a period of time, local administrators acquired a certain amount of de facto
autonomy with a minimum of surveillance. For example, a survey of the local press and decisions
of the Leningrad Executive Committee during the
1950's as compared to more recent years shows a
greater variety and greater initiative in local
regulations and only an occasional reference to

central directives. In contrast to Stalin, his successors decided that the needs of consumers and
citizens could no longer be ignored as unessentials,
and they began to administer to these needs centrally. Thus, a comparison of the authority of Leningrad's city government in 1950, 1956, and 1961 indicates that local leaders have lost a great deal
of their de facto autonomy and have become agents
of the central government and propaganda mouth-
pieces for the central Party leadership. On the
basis of the published records, only 6 per cent of
the Executive Committee's decisions in 1950 were
passed in response to directives from above, while
in 1956 the proportion rose to 17 per cent, and in
1961, to 32 per cent. Although the evidence is not
conclusive and does not preclude the existence of a
large number of unpublicized directives in 1950,
the current public emphasis on mass participation
and local administration would seem to indicate
greater reasons to cover up centralized directives
today than in the past. At the same time, the role
of local government as an instrument of propaganda
has increased. While for 1950 there is no record
of the Executive Committee and the city soviet
passing a joint resolution with the Party or trade
unions, in 1956 one joint resolution was passed
with the unions; in 1961, 17 per cent of the published resolutions (primarily of a propaganda nature) were issued jointly with the Party or trade
unions. That the city government has increasingly
become an instrument of propaganda can also be seen
in the increase of purely sloganized decisions.
The proportion rose from 6 per cent of the published
decisions in 1950 to 11 per cent in 1956, and 29
per cent in 1961. Thus, in spite of Khrushchev's
declarations about decentralization in matters of
local government, the reverse seems to be true.

In addition to coordinating local activities,
the Party's other main function is supervision of
the local government on behalf of the central
authorities, and, in theory, on behalf of the population. As stated above, appointments to all city
posts are screened by the local Party organs,

although for numerous positions nominated by a republic ministry, this is often probably a mere
formality. Furthermore, at least 75 per cent of
the chiefs and assistant chiefs of the city departments are Party members and individually are sub-
ject to Party discipline.| Party control is further
strengthened by the fact that from early youth the
Soviet administrator has received a highly politicized education in the schools and Party organizations, and he is sensitive to shifts in the Party
line. He knows exactly how he is expected to re-
spond, and, furthermore, he knows he is powerless
to pick a quarrel with the Party unless he is
assured of powerful backing from Moscow.

The Party organs also contain departments that
have a special supervisory role, and the Party administrators from these departments at both the
city and provincial level are found on several of
the city's coordinating committees. | Soviet studies
on local government and administration say very
little or nothing about the relationship of the
Party to government, and works on the Party are
vague as to the actual powers of supervision. It
is known, however, that the Party often becomes
directly engaged in the administrative process itself, because Party organs are constantly being
admonished for becoming so involved that they weaken
their supervisory role. Because the Party can so
easily take over the administrative process, it
would seem to indicate that in most cases it has
extensive powers and can at least issue cease and
desist orders.| Beginning around 1960, Khrushchev,
in an effort to advance the Party's role, ordered
Party agencies to take a more direct hand in administration. This was made explicit in the 1961
Party statutes and in the 1962 Party reorganization
into agricultural and industrial sectors. Since
Khrushchev's fall, however, the Party has been ordered to return to its traditional, ambiguous role
of supervision.

Charts 3 and 4 show Party organization at the
oblast and city levels. In each of the fourteen

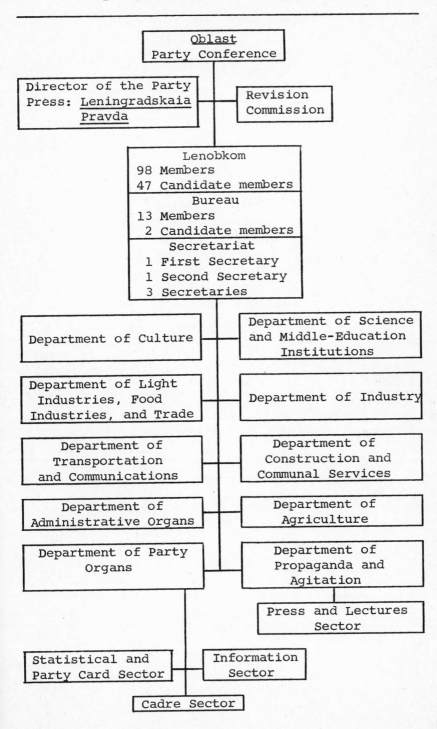

CHART 3

Party Departments at the <u>Oblast</u> Level

Oblast
Party Conference

Director of the Party
Press: <u>Leningradskaia
Pravda</u>

Revision
Commission

Lenobkom
98 Members
47 Candidate members
Bureau
13 Members
2 Candidate members
Secretariat
1 First Secretary
1 Second Secretary
3 Secretaries

Department of Culture

Department of Science
and Middle-Education
Institutions

Department of Light
Industries, Food
Industries, and Trade

Department of Industry

Department of
Transportation
and Communications

Department of
Construction and
Communal Services

Department of
Administrative Organs

Department of
Agriculture

Department of Party
Organs

Department of
Propaganda and
Agitation

Press and Lectures
Sector

Statistical and
Party Card Sector

Information
Sector

Cadre Sector

CHART 4

Party Departments at the City Level

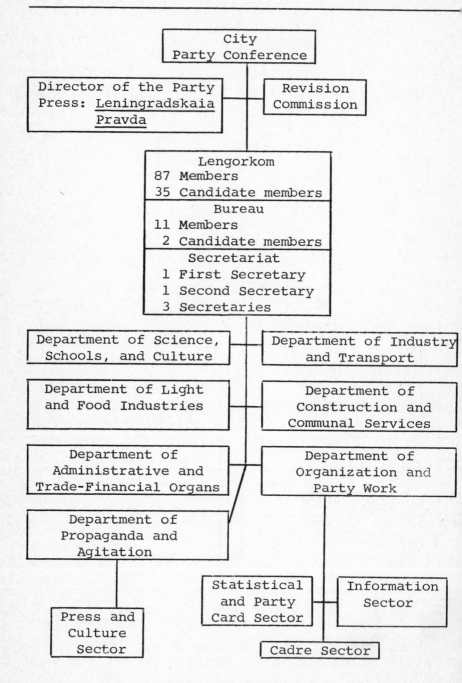

City
Party Conference

Director of the Party
Press: Leningradskaia
Pravda

Revision
Commission

Lengorkom
87 Members
35 Candidate members
Bureau
11 Members
2 Candidate members
Secretariat
1 First Secretary
1 Second Secretary
3 Secretaries

Department of Science,
Schools, and Culture

Department of Industry
and Transport

Department of Light
and Food Industries

Department of
Construction and
Communal Services

Department of
Administrative and
Trade-Financial Organs

Department of
Organization and
Party Work

Department of
Propaganda and
Agitation

Press and
Culture
Sector

Statistical
and Party
Card Sector

Information
Sector

Cadre Sector

rayons of the city proper, moreover, the Party organ has three departments: organization, propaganda and agitation, and industry and transport.

Working closely with the Party departments at
all three levels are the permanent Party commissions, made up of Party activists, including some
rank-and-file members from primary organizations.
For example, the Commission on Technical Progress
is divided into five to seven working sections for
various fields. A presidium of fifteen to twenty
members plans the work of the Commission. This
presidium represents the Commission's sections,
the Party secretariat, the Komsomols (youth groups),
and the Party department on industry and transportation. A plenary session of the entire Commission
is held two or three times a year, and the sections
meet once a month.

All three levels of the Party (oblast, city,
and rayon) also have under their direction commissions of people's control whose job it is to maintain the excellence and legality of the government.
Prior to 1962 there had existed two separate hier-
archies--Commissions of Party Control attached to
the Central Committee of the Party and Commissions
of State Control attached to the U.S.S.R. Council
of Ministers. In 1962 they were combined into one
powerful system of Organs of Party-State Control.
But in 1965 the new leadership--fearing the power
of this hierarchy and its leader, Alexander
Shelepin--reorganized it into a new system of
Organs of People's Control. They have been separ-
ated from the Party and are elected. Nevertheless,
their activities are directed and normally led by
one of the local Party secretaries. Subordinate
to these commissions in Leningrad are 5,400 people's
control groups in the city's departments and enterprises. The actual role and authority of these
commissions and groups are still in doubt because
a new statute providing for their activities has
not been passed.

It is impossible to judge the extent of

corruption in local government because there are no
crime statistics, and only occasionally does the
press report an incident of bribery or embezzlement.
Given all the checks, particularly financial checks,
corruption is not easy to carry out, and the puri-
tanism of the ideology is still sufficiently strong
that the practice is frowned upon by society. The
general impression held by Leningrad's citizens
seems to be that the local administration is often
bureaucratic but not generally corrupt. Nevertheless, a friend in the administrative apparatus can
be very helpful in getting things done. The citizen or lower government official who does not have
blat (influence) or who is not a member of the in-
group is frustrated by negative answers and re-
stricting regulations and finds that it is difficult, if not impossible, to get anywhere with the
bureaucracy. The mass agitation work of the Party
together with the city government and trade unions
will be discussed in a later section on "Mass Participation in Local Government."

ADMINISTRATIVE DEPARTMENTS

Functionally the Leningrad city government is
broken down into more than thirty basic divisions
of different types. (See the formally designated
city departments and managements marked with an
asterisk in Chart 2.) The Soviets use a variety of
designations for these subdivisions, as seen in
Chart 2. The terms used are: department, chief
management, management, and bureau. Although in
formal lists the subdivisions of city government
are put in order of rank, with the chief managements at the top, in practice, the various terms
offer little key to the actual authority or prestige of a subdivision. For the sake of simplicity,
we shall refer to all of them as departments, except for the special committees and institutes that
are not formally listed as separate divisions of
local government.

The heads of all the departments are also

deputies of the city soviet and are formally elected
to their positions in the same way that the Executive Committee is theoretically elected by the
soviet. From all the evidence, it is clear that
they are appointed by a central ministry or the
Presidium of the city soviet, with a screening by
the Party apparatus. Then a constituency is found
for each, so that they can be elected to the city
soviet. Finally, at the first meeting of the
soviet, they are elected to head their designated
departments. Interim changes in chiefs of departments can be made by the Executive Committee of
the Soviet.

⌐The departments of Finance, Security,   A
Architect-Planning, Construction Materials, Education, and Construction are branches of union-
republic ministries. The directives of these departments come entirely from central authorities
as do their finances, although in some cases they
are included in the local budget as a matter of
form. Nevertheless, as departments within the
jurisdiction of the Leningrad Soviet, they are
supposed to coordinate their activities with the
local government.⌐In some instances, local   B
branches have the task of supervising local authorities, as, for example, the Finance Department,
which must approve all financial transactions, or
the Architect-Planning Department, which must approve all new construction in the city regardless
of the source.⌡

⌐The department chiefs appointed by the cen-   C
tral authorities (but formally elected) are powerful figures who are usually appointed to the Executive Committee. (See Table 6.) As key personnel
in the power structure, they are frequently members of the city Party committee (Lengorkom) and
various coordinating committees as well.⌡ In 1967,
for example, the head of the Education Department
was on the Audit Commission of the city Party committee. The chiefs of the departments of Trade,
Architect-Planning, Construction, and Security are
members or candidate members of the Lengorkom.

TABLE 6

Department Heads in the Leningrad
Executive Committee, 1948-65

Department	Number of Terms on the Committee
Education	9
Finance	9
Trade	9
Architect-Planning	8
Construction	8
Housing	7
Roads and Bridges	6
Tram-Trolley	6
Construction Materials	4
Public Health	3
Water and Sewage	2
Gas Economy	2
Local Industry	2
Communal Enterprises	2
Security	2

Source: Compiled by author.

A second group of departments, which includes A
Social Security, General Food Supplies, Communal
and Domestic Services, Culture, Fuel Supplies, the
Press, Radio-Television, Local Industries, Bread
Industries, and Trade, are also attached to central
ministries. But these departments are also in practice responsible to the local soviet, and the city
Executive Committee appears to have some discretion
in the nomination of the chiefs of these departments.

A third group of departments deals with func- B
tions over which central authorities exercise only
general supervision. These include departments of
Gas Supplies, Roads and Bridges, Water and Sewage,
Housing, Housing Allocation, and Accounting, Capital
Repairs, Movie Theaters, Parks and Gardens, Tram-
Trolleybus, Local Water Transport, and Subway
Management. The Executive Committee fully controls
these departments in detail, including their budgets. The profits from these enterprises make up
an important part of the city's income. Some of
the more important of these departments, such as
Housing, Roads and Bridges, and Tram-Trolleybus
are normally represented on the Executive Committee.

A fourth group of departments performs ser- C
vices and coordinating functions for the Executive
Committee and the other departments. These include the departments of Internal Relations, General Affairs, the Archives, Organization-Instruction,
Supplies, Technical Management, Cadres, and Training.
The Department of General Affairs serves primarily
as the secretariat for the Executive Committee and
its Presidium. The Department of Organization-
Instruction and the Department of Internal Affairs
coordinate the activities of the rayon governments.
In addition, the inspection corps of the Organization-
Instruction Department investigates the work of those
departments over which city and rayon governments
have primary control. The inspection corps is broken
down into five sectors:

1. Construction, capital repairs, and housing administration

2.   Trade and general provisions

3.   Daily and communal services

4.   Welfare, transport, and communications

5.   Social and cultural questions.

Activists from the general population are recruited
as auxiliary inspectors. Although the Organization-
Instruction Department is the primary inspection
agency for the city, it is but one of several agencies constantly investigating local government.⌋

A final group of departments, committees, and
institutes is not listed in the formal roster of
city executive departments. These agencies number
somewhere between twenty-five and fifty. The exact
number is impossible to determine, because several
are attached to major departments but have separate
functions and are partially autonomous. Thus, the
group includes the arbitration tribunals which are
autonomous bodies elected by the city soviet to
arbitrate contract disputes between local enterprises. For general directives, they look to the
arbitration tribunals at the republic level, but
their administration is under the general supervision of the Presidium of the Executive Committee
and particularly its first vice-chairman. This
group also includes Lenproekt, which is an institute under the Architect-Planning Department that
produces detailed working drawings for that department and independent work for others (such as the
Department of Garden and Parks and the Department
of Capital Repairs), and even accepts assignments
from other cities. Still another type of organization in this group is gorvoenkomat, which is a committee with its own staff to plan civil defense.
It operates under the chairman of the Presidium and
works jointly with the army and navy commanders in
the area. The activities of this heterogeneous
group of agencies are coordinated through the Presidium and its members.⌋ For the division of responsibility among the members, see Chart 2.

Manipulating and changing the administrative structure for improved efficiency is a favorite device of Soviet leaders at all levels, and this addiction to change is very evident in Leningrad. A year does not go by without the disappearance of one or more departments and the creation of new ones. The unstable character of the structure has been particularly marked recently, primarily as a result of the process of decentralization and recentralization of the economy since 1957. For example, from 1963 to 1965, during the period of recentralization of the economy, the departments of local industry, light industry, and wood and forest industries were abolished in the city, and many of the enterprises formerly under them were placed under the direct authority of the republic ministries of Light Industry and Forest Industry. Then, in January, 1966, the Department of Local Industry was re-established and twenty-four factories previously under the Leningrad Sovnarkhoz,[6] which was being dissolved, were turned over to the new department. In the same time period and apart from the effects of recentralization, additional changes occurred. Printing enterprises in the city's various departments were reorganized not once but twice; some five or six new coordination committees were created; and at least four departments changed status.

Instability is not only common to the departmental structure but is also common for department leadership and membership on the Executive Committee. Of all the persons who served on the Leningrad Executive Committee or who headed one of the departments between 1948 and 1966, 60 per cent served only a single two-year term. No one held office throughout the entire period, and only 6 of a total of 182 chief administrators served 6 two-year terms. The turnover of department heads, on the one hand, and on the Executive Committee and Presidium, on the other hand, was about equal, indicative that instability is a general phenomenon among all the top ranks of the city government. There is insufficient evidence to say how far down the hierarchy this general turnover is prevalent,

but scraps of circumstantial evidence indicate it
may affect at least the second rank.   Turnover in
the city of Leningrad is similar to that in Moscow
but not as great as that in Leningrad Oblast, which
seems to have been particularly hard hit by purges.
(See Table 7.)   The posts that suffer the least from
turnover in personnel are of two types: first, a
few of the more technical positions and, secondly,
ministerial appointments, the departments of
Architect-Planning, Finance, and Education.   The
ability of D. I. Petrikeev to remain head of the
Education Department from 1950 to 1962 is particularly noteworthy, because the regime initiated several educational reforms in that period which, following the usual Soviet practice, means the leaders
associated with the old system should have been removed.   Furthermore, one would think de-Stalinizatio
of the bureaucracy would certainly have affected the
educational system.   Yet Stalin's appointees were
very much in evidence in the education departments
of both Leningrad and Moscow in the 1960's.

TABLE 7

Turnover of High-Ranking Officials in
Local Government, 1948-62

	% Elected More than Twice	Average Number of Terms in Office
Leningrad	29	1.87
Moscow	29	1.99
Leningrad Oblast	19	1.63

Source: Compiled by author.

Given the volatile political situation in the
Soviet Union from the last years of Stalin to the
supremacy of Khrushchev, it is not surprising that
there were some periods of more rapid turnover.

In Leningrad, the evidence indicates that cycles of
turnover in high level personnel occurred at different times from that in Moscow. In the period
1948-51, there was almost a complete changeover in
Leningrad with the purging of the Zhdanov supporters
by Malenkov, leaving only five of the old officeholders unaffected. (See Table 8.) No such house-
cleaning occurred in Moscow. Changes of lesser mag-
nitude were evident in Leningrad after 1953 and
1959, while changeovers occurred in Moscow in 1952
and again after 1957. Even between purges, however, the rate of holdover was only about 60 per
cent after each election. The removal of Khrushchev
in 1964 did not cause any major personnel shift in
either Moscow or Leningrad, as it did not among
leaders at the national level.

TABLE 8

Turnover of Top Government Personnel*
for the City of Leningrad, 1948-65

Term	Turnover %
1948-51	90
1951-53	34
1953-55	40
1955-57	24
1957-59	29
1959-61	42
1961-63	32
1963-65	32

*Includes members of the Presidium, Executive
Committee, and heads of departments.

Source: Compiled by author.

The surprising factor about the turnover of personnel is that it should have affected a majority of those departmental chiefs who were relatively removed from the center of politics. (See Table 9.) Apart from those on the Executive Committee of the city soviet, none of the other department heads serve as members of top Party committees in Leningrad. Although they are Party members, they are primarily professional administrators and technicians, a step removed from the main stream of politics. The reasons for the turnover within the technician category seem to be twofold. First, the shifting of personnel as well as departments is the generally accepted means of trying to improve the administrative system. Second, frequent transfer of personnel is considered the best way of preventing the buildup of power cliques and of keeping administrators on their toes. The frequent reports in the press of sabotage of the new reforms by the entrenched Ministry of Finance and its local departments illustrate the danger of long tenure.

TABLE 9

Length in Office of Presidium Members,
Executive Committee, and Department
Heads, Leningrad, 1948-66

	Total No. of Individuals	Years in Office							
		2	4	6	8	10	12	14	16
Presidium members	32	11	8	7	4	1	1		
Executive Committee members	75	49	10	6	1	5	1	2	1
Department heads*	96	47	18	12	10	5	1	2	1
Total	203	107	36	25	15	11	3	4	2

*Includes only those department heads not also serving on the Executive Committee.

Source: Compiled by author.

The Soviet Union has always publicized the
role women play in government activities. The
propaganda points out that about 40 per cent of the
members of the local soviets are women, with 41.7
per cent in the Leningrad soviets in 1961. But because election to a soviet is an honor without ac-
companying political power, such a figure is not
significant. Of more significance is the fact that
women comprise only about 10 per cent of the membership of Executive Committees, the Presidiums and
department heads in the cities of Leningrad and
Moscow and in the Leningrad Oblast. Furthermore,
there is no indication that over the last fifteen
years their role has increased. Currently there
are three women on the Leningrad Executive Committee, one of whom is a vice-chairman, and there are
no women heads of executive departments. The women
seem to do better in the Party organization, and
21 out of 107 Party secretaries of rayon and city
organizations in Leningrad were women in 1964.

RAYON GOVERNMENTS

The fourteen urban and five suburban rayons of
Leningrad are wards of the city, and their boundaries are frequently changed. The city can change
the boundaries and numbers of rayons with the permission of the Presidium of the supreme soviet of
the R.S.F.S.R. In principle, the purpose is to
keep the urban rayons integral areas of about
25,000 acres with 300,000 to 400,000 people. In
their governmental structure, the rayons are small
replicas of the city, except that their executive
committees have no presidiums, and there are fewer
departments, each of which is directly subordinate
to a corresponding city department. Each rayon has
an elected soviet of about 230 deputies and an executive committee of about fifteen. Each rayon has
its own planning commission and budget, but all
plans, expenditures, and revenues are approved by
the city and form a part of the city's budget. The
sizes of rayon budgets range from 9 to 17 million
rubles.

The rayon governments in general operate as local offices of the city for the following purposes

1. Housing--distribution, repairs, and management of housing

2. Medical services--neighborhood clinics, hospitals, and rest homes

3. Social security--payments for invalids, unemployment, and pensions

4. Education--nursery schools, crèches, schools for adults,and mass education

5. Culture and recreation--local libraries, cultural clubs, and sports organizations

6. Rayon parks and gardens

7. Food distribution--local restaurants, food stores, and collective-farm markets

8. Public services--laundries, public baths, cleaners, barbers, and repair shops for shoes, clothing, furniture, etc.

In every case the corresponding city department closely supervises the activities of the rayon department. Furthermore, the city's organization-instruction department acts as the special liaison organization between the city and rayons. It directs the general activities of the rayon government, particularly the work of the executive committees and rayon soviets. It trains rayon personnel and maintains a corps of inspectors to insure the proper functioning of services.

In addition to the division of the city into rayons, within the boundaries of the five suburban rayons and subject to their supervision, are local soviets of eighteen towns (four of which are classified as cities) and numerous workers' settlements. Moreover, the city rayons are broken down

for both administrative and planning purposes into
living rayons, microrayons, and blocks of residential houses. Further, for such communal services
as water, sewage, heating, and electricity the city
is broken down into separate districts. (These
various subdivisions are discussed in detail in
Chapter 4.)

RECRUITMENT OF PERSONNEL FOR CITY GOVERNMENT

The Leningrad city government with its various
services and enterprises employs almost 400,000
people. The vast majority are unionized, but there
is no single civil service system of recruitment or
promotion. There are no central labor exchanges or
employment offices for recruitment of city employees.
Instead, each department has set up its own scheme,
based on directives of the department's supervisory
agency, albeit a central ministry or local government. For strictly local organs, personnel schemes
are established by the Executive Committee of the
city under the over-all supervision and directives
of the R.S.F.S.R. Council of Ministers or the Ministry of Communal Economy. Salary schedules and
job descriptions are entirely controlled by the republic and All-Union governments. In general, the
salaries of local government personnel are scaled
slightly lower than those in light industry and
are significantly lower than those in heavy and
defense industries. This low salary scale and the
resulting low status of city personnel create a
serious problem of turnover and a permanent bias
in the system against local government. (Its effect on housing is discussed in Chapter 5.) In
the lower ranks of the hierarchy, hiring is ad hoc;
little attempt is made to recruit on a regular,
competitive basis. In recent years, in particular,
it has been difficult to find enough qualified
people to fill positions, and there is widespread
advertising for clerks and workers. The city departments do make special efforts to recruit new
graduates from the school system, but most of these

recruits, if they are at all capable, after a year
of experience find higher paying jobs in industry.
Recruitment of higher-level administrators is also
somewhat haphazard, although the city works closely
with the University of Leningrad and other local institutions of higher learning. Many of the top administrative personnel are recruited from the law
faculty of the University, as is common in contin-
ental Europe. The law faculty offers courses and
seminars in the theory of public administration and
even has a specialized department on administrative
law. The formal training is entirely theoretical,
committing to memory the ideal concepts of social-
istic administration. In class, no attempt is made
to deal with the practical problems of administration. Probably the most important part of the program, therefore, is the inservice training provided
students in the law faculty. During at least part
of the summer, the students are assigned to work in
the courts or some local government bureau. While
they must report in some detail on their summer's
work to their adviser, no attempt is made to integrate their formal training with their practical
experience. Also, many clerks and administrators
in the middle and lower ranks of local government
take correspondence courses or attend night school
in the law or other faculties of the University.
In 1963-64, compared to the University's day school
enrollment of 7,820 students, there were 4,640 evening students and 4,152 students in correspondence
courses. Other institutions of higher learning in
Leningrad also have a large enrollment in evening
and correspondence courses. Successful completion
of a degree automatically qualifies a clerk or administrator for a major promotion and/or a salary
raise. The Soviet system is very degree conscious.

MASS PARTICIPATION IN LOCAL GOVERNMENT

The Soviet theory of government has always
stressed the role of the masses in supervising and
even participating in the operation of government.
Popular participation was given renewed emphasis

with the drafting of the new program of the Communist Party in 1959-60, which stressed the transition to Communism and greater participation of the
masses as part of the withering away of the state
apparatus. Because local government is close to
the people and the least politically and economical-
ly important to the power ambitions among top leadership, it is this area that has had the most experimentation with popular participation. Soviet
literature is full of exhortations to local officials to try new ways of drawing the masses into
administration in the form of so-called public organizations. When working with local administrators,
however, it is clear that they view the public's
role in a different light and are acting only under
pressure. Instead, they see participation by the
masses mostly as a burden and at best as a source
of free and extra labor to fulfill the city's goals.

The city soviets and the rayon soviets have
always been considered primary vehicles of citizenship participation. In the city and rayon soviets,
there are 5,836 deputies, of which 58 per cent are
Party members or candidates for membership. Elections to these soviets are held every two years,
and it is considered a virtue that a large proportion are elected for the first time. In 1965, 376
(62 per cent) of the members of the city soviet
were elected for the first time; in the rayon
soviets, 2,561 (59 per cent) were elected for the
first time. Neither the large number nor the turnover of deputies has much effect on the city government, but the constant infusion of new members is
considered essential for mobilizing the population
behind local government. Within the administrative
apparatus of the city government, it is the primary
responsibility of the Organization-Instruction Department to organize mass activities, to train
deputies, and to help them organize community activities through the permanent commissions of the
rayon and city soviets and other mass committees.

Party pressure for widespread popular participation since 1957-58 has led to a series of new

and renewed ventures into mass agitation and participation.   The first step was to revitalize the
permanent commissions attached to the city and
rayon soviets. (See Charts 5 and 6.)   These commissions, composed of about twenty members drawn
from the soviets and elected by them, are to check
and report on various activities in local governmen
In Leningrad, 4,630 deputies are on commissions for
rayon and city soviets.   In addition, some 27,000
activists are reported to have been recruited from
the population to help in the investigations.   Although these commissions existed under Stalin, in
practice they were usually moribund.   The current
line is to give them new life.   Because their purpose is to serve as an independent check on the executive, theoretically they are responsible only to
their soviets and not to the executive committees;
heads of executive departments are forbidden to
serve on them.   They meet once a month for seven
or eight months of the year.   Periodically they
present reports to the soviets on the operations
of one or more of the executive departments, and
they make suggestions for changes in various city
regulations and operations.   From personal observa-
tion of their activities, it becomes clear that
both the independence and the extensive operations
of these commissions remain largely fictitious.
Their reports, instead of being products of the
commissions, are often the joint efforts of the
head of the executive department under investigation and the secretariat of the commission.   The
commission secretariat is supplied by the
Organization-Instruction Department attached to
the Executive Committee of the city and subject to
its authority.   The role of the interested citizen
in the commission is even more minimal and perfunctory than that of the deputy member.   There is
little evidence that the commissions or their reports play a very important role in helping to
draft legislation.   Occasionally, the leadership
does choose to use a permanent commission to ex-
pose the shortcomings of a department or to build
up propaganda support for new regulations.   At
most, the permanent commission is useful to the

CHART 5

Permanent Commissions of the Leningrad City Soviet

Budget
Communal Services
Construction and Construction Materials
Culture
Fuel and Energy
Housing
Industry
People's Education
Public Health
Social Security
Socialist Legality and Social Order
Trade and Food Supplies
Transport and Communications
Welfare and Security

CHART 6

Typical Permanent Commissions of Rayon
  Soviets Within the City of Leningrad*

Administrative Legality
Budget
Communal and Daily Services
Construction
Culture
Housing
People's Education
Public Health and Social Security
Public Welfare
Trade and General Provisions

---

*Permanent rayon commissions are often headed
by deputies of the city soviet, thus providing for
central direction.

Executive Committee as an occasional semi-independent
check on the activities of a department and as a complaint center for registering popular dissatisfaction

Another major organization in the area of mass
agitation and mobilization is the local council of
trade unions. While the primary task of trade
unions in the Soviet Union is to act as agents of
the state in advancing industrial production, they
also have extensive responsibility for expressing
the daily needs of the population. In Leningrad,
90 per cent of the workers and service personnel belong to trade unions, a total of about 1.5 million
members in the city. The trade unions are organized into 96,000 brigades. Virtually all resolutions of the city soviet dealing with mass agitation and organization, socialist competition, and
designating outstanding workers are signed by the
chairman of the Executive Committee, the secretary
of the Oblast Trade-Union Council, and usually the
first secretary of the city Party committee. For
example, every three months the Leningrad Party
Bureau, the Presidium of the Leningrad Oblast Council of Trade Unions, and the Executive Committee
of the city issue a joint statement on the fulfillment of plans for the previous quarter and identify
the tasks for the next quarter. Furthermore, the
trade unions are assigned a primary role in carrying out joint resolutions. The subordinate character of the trade unions in carrying out the command
of the government and Party in the U.S.S.R. was
firmly established in the early 1930's.

Similar to the dual role played by the permanent commissions, trade unions also serve as another popular check on the activities of local government, including the fulfillment of the plan and
observance of legal norms. For example, the Presidium of the Leningrad Oblast Central Committee
of Trade Unions appoints several groups of inspectors to check on the construction of new housing
and housing repairs in the city. Representatives
of the trade union are also included on all of the
city's various coordinating committees. Thus, the

trade unions are an integral part of local government, participating in the administrative decisions
of the government, mobilizing the masses behind the
government, and checking on the activities of government administrators. But the very subordinate
character of the trade unions to Party and government leaders makes them in fact ineffective policy-
makers and agents of investigation.

    In all-out support for popular participation,
considered a sign of the transition to Communism,
the local soviets, trade unions, and Party organs
of Leningrad began organizing and recruiting the
population into proliferating so-called volunteer
organizations in the areas of education, housing,
retail trade, sanitation, culture, parks, police,
justice, and so forth. Like other cities, Leningrad followed the Soviet tradition of playing the
numbers game with these organs, boasting that it
had 20,000 volunteer organizations and included
450,000 persons. Of these groups, there are 1,726
druzhini units (citizens' groups to maintain public
order), with 55,000 persons participating; 1,211
comradely courts with 8,586 members; 1,780 housing
committees and 205 street committees with 30,000
activists, and so on ad infinitum. A large portion
of the participants are Party members. For example,
out of some 55,000 druzhini, 30,000 belong to the
Party. Upon investigating a few of these public
organizations, the membership was found lacking in
enthusiasm and initiative. It is quite obvious
that the city administration has used the organizations to do some of its unpleasant tasks and has
used them as a source of free labor. Soviet writers freely praise the economic savings to the system, pointing out that Leningrad planted trees at
no cost and that the city government was able to
complete a 50,000 ruble repair job for 6,000 rubles
with the use of volunteer labor. In addition to
reducing expenses, the city fathers found that the
social pressures applied by the druzhini and comradely courts were often more effective in disci-
plining the population than were the regular militia
and courts. Similarly, by permitting the housing

committees to deal with the unpleasant duty of maintaining discipline among the tenants and by turning
over to trade-union committees the responsibility
for distribution of scarce housing, the city government escapes embarrassment and unpopularity. Furthe
more, the Party not infrequently makes use of the
volunteer organs as a means to chastise local author
ities.

Another role that mass organizations are to
assume increasingly as the Soviet Union moves toward its goals of communist society is the direct
administration of government functions. Leningrad
has boasted of initiative in this area. By 1962,
at the rayon level, there were forty so-called nonstaff sectors run by citizens' groups, including
cultural departments, departments of inspection
and instruction, and an occasional retail outlet.
Out of a total of 359 instructors and inspectors
in city and rayon government, 325 were nonstaff and
unpaid. Most of these unpaid workers were recruited
among pensioners. Although the total impact of
these volunteer workers has been minor and although
they have played a subordinate role, on occasion
they have become a source of conflict. In particular, the councils of pensioners have had a tendency
to get out of hand, and it has been necessary in
some cases to dissolve them.

Since the dismissal of Khrushchev in 1964,
there has been a decline in mass participation in
government. Lip service is still given to the
idea, and the trade unions are still an important
link with the masses. But these so-called volunteer groups, so numerous in 1962-64, were much less
numerous by 1966, and their activities had also declined. Furthermore, resolutions of the Executive
Committee in 1965 complained that the druzhini
were understaffed by 70 to 80 per cent, many permanent commissions of the rayons were not meeting,
and comradely courts were meeting only once a quarter. The effort to keep them active in the face
of disinterest by so much of the population apparently had not been worth the work that it produced.

Another channel of citizen participation is
the daily newspaper. Letters-to-the-editor columns
of the morning and evening papers are important
means of registering citizens' complaints against
improper activities of local government. Occasionally, local complaints are even published in the
national press. Some writers in the West have argued that the letters of complaint are inspired
and contrived by the leadership, but from our evidence, this does not always seem to be true. Particularly among the more educated, a letter to the
editor is considered a useful and legitimate channel of complaint. Undoubtedly the letters are,
however, carefully screened and only those approved
by the Party are published. Once published, these
letters are taken seriously and call for some kind
of investigation and a published response by local
governmental authorities.

CONCLUSION

In addition to the extensive and continuous
control exercised by Moscow over local government,
two other features of Soviet local government stand
out in this case study of Leningrad. One is the
maze of control and inspection organs that grew up
in the period of the First Five-Year Plan (1928-32)
and persists today. All of the basic institutions
operating at the local level are active in control
roles. Some of the coordinating and control devices used by these units are discussed above, and
subsequent chapters enumerate others. As discussed
above, the more important include the inspecting
and coordinating bureaus and committees of the
city government itself, corresponding organs of
the Party and trade unions, permanent commissions
of the local soviets, mass organs, and central inspection and control agencies such as the banks,
Gosplan, the Finance Department, and the people's
control commissions. The channels are so overwhelming and numerous that they are confusing and
often contradictory. What is even more significant
is the fact that the multiplicity of controls has

become an accepted feature of Soviet life.   Its
basic value is never challenged, and only certain
peripheral aspects of the system are criticized.
Proposed solutions call for greater discretion in
decision-making, but rarely is any thought given to
cutting back on the maze of control organs.   From
the Western observer's point of view, the amount
and frequency of checks are a gross waste of manpower and effort.   That even the smallest transac-
tion, for example, must be approved and checked
three or four times seems like gross inefficiency.
It appears all the more ridiculous to the Western
observer when it is evident that at least half the
checking devices are merely a matter of formality
and that the other half fail to check important
features such as quality of performance.

As stated in later chapters, even the Soviets
are generally dissatisfied with the control operation, but their suggestions call for expanding or
strengthening control agencies, rarely for reducing
them.   It is also evident to the observer that all
of this checking tends to stifle initiative and in-
novation because the system provides so little leeway, even with the liberalization of the 1960's.
Soviet economists are only beginning to recognize
this problem with respect to industry, but there
is no discussion of this problem as yet with respect to government administration.   In fact, in
areas such as housing, the trend is toward increased controls.   Furthermore, such powerful control organs as the Finance Department are entrenched
and conservative.   The Ministry of Finance has frequently held back administrative reforms even when
approved by top leadership.

A   General Soviet texts on administration never
discuss the problems of red tape and confusion.
Rather, they praise the superiority of socialist
administration over capitalist bureaucracy.   Yet
even a cursory reading of the daily press as well
as articles and letters in the professional journals points up the failure of control and coordination as a major shortcoming of local administration

The constant reorganization of the system by its
leaders is another indication of this problem.

The second feature of note that stands out in   A
our analysis of Leningrad's local government is the
widespread dependence on personal relations. They
are the primary means by which the mazes of organs
and counterorgans achieve some unity of direction
and by which disputes are settled. Even so, an appeal to Moscow to settle a dispute is not uncommon.
In any discussion of the problem of coordination
with government officials, it is quite clear that
more reliance is placed on personal relationships
not only with Moscow but within the city government than on all the coordinating committees. For
example, a telephone call or a personal note between the chairmen of the Executive Committee and
the Leningrad Economic Region (Lensovnarkhoz) during its short history, 1957-64, settled most of
the problems that came up between the two organs.
In the same way, the head of the Architect-Planning
Department is able to expedite approval for construction of buildings through his personal contacts
in Moscow.

It must also be noted that in general Leningrad's special position has allowed it to escape
some of the worst Soviet red tape and confusion.
In the first place, the city of Leningrad has
direct legal access to the R.S.F.S.R. Council of
Ministers and is not required to channel its appeal to Moscow through an oblast government.
Second, the top leaders in the Leningrad Party and
government, and particularly the First Party-
Secretary of Leningrad, are important personages
in the Soviet political system, with direct access
to ministers and Party officials in Moscow, both
at the republic and All-Union levels. Finally, as   B
discussed in Chapters 4 and 5, the Leningrad city
government has, from the beginning, controlled most
of its communal services and has not had to dispute with various enterprises in the area over this
responsibility. In this regard it is even better
off than Moscow, where buildings and housing come

under the direct control of over 200 different departments and ministries of the All-Union and Rus-
sian Republic governments.|

For the average citizen in Leningrad, the
direct pay-off is the fact that the city's trade
outlets are comparatively well stocked, and crucial
items are rarely in short supply, while in many
smaller cities this is a constant complaint. In
fact, not only do travelers stock up there, but
the people of Leningrad send scarce items to rela-
tives and friends elsewhere in the U.S.S.R.

But even if Leningrad has certain advantages
in being able to cut some red tape, it still wastes
much effort in futile checks and inspections of inspections. It is doubtful, furthermore, whether
red tape in the lower echelons of the bureaucracy
dealing with the citizens is any less in Leningrad
than in other Russian cities. By most Western
standards it is considerable and time consuming.
Spravkas (permission slips) and numerous signatures
are the norm. In the area of services operated by
the city, inconveniences are uneven. For example,
it takes over a month to get shoes repaired, but
within twenty-four hours of a request, someone will
come to fix a television set, although the quality
of the repair is sometimes questionable.

Thus, in spite of the authority and flexibility possible under the Soviet socialist system of
government, Leningrad's government is cumbersome
and dependent on the whims of central authorities,
and its improvement over the city administrations
that have evolved haphazardly in many Western
cities is doubtful. The next chapter will discuss
the various types of city planning, a field in
which the Soviet regime claims special prowess.

NOTES TO CHAPTER 2

1.   Izvestiia, April 3, 1962.

2.   In 1959 Isaev was appointed Chief of the
Housing, Civil and Industrial Construction Department and in 1961 became a First Vice-Chairman of
the Executive Committee before becoming Chairman.

3.   In the Soviet Union, the naming of streets
and parks after deceased leaders is a very sensitive and political subject. Each of these leaders
has a current status that must be carefully respected.

4.   Voprosi partiinogo stroitelstva [Questions
of Party Structure] (Leningrad, 1965), p. 200. In
the city there are 4,500 primary Party organizations,
5,500 shop organizations, and 13,000 Party groups;
V. A. Berezov, V partiinuiu rabotu [In Party Work]
(Leningrad, 1964), p. 4.

5.   Jerry Hough, "The Soviet Elite II," Problems of Communism (March-April, 1967), pp. 11, 18-25.

6.   The Leningrad Sovnarkhoz was the economic
region created in 1957 for Leningrad and the surrounding oblast.

CHAPTER **3** PLANNING

PLANS IN A VARIETY OF FORMS

A   As is true in Western cities, Leningrad's primary operating plan is an annual budget, which controls the city's over-all recurrent expenditures.
B But this is only one of several plans that affect the city. Each of the city's enterprises and departments, particularly those which are engaged in production, distribution, or selling, has an annual plan that includes indices for output, productivity,
C profit, a wage fund, and similar matters. These are combined into one over-all production plan for the city and are approved both locally and by Mos-
D cow. There is also the city's separate yearly construction plan that provides for new buildings and capital repairs.

     Besides the annually based plans, there are a
E variety of plans with different time spans. The yearly plans, for example, are broken down into quarters, and checks on the fulfillment of each quarterly plan serve as an important control mechanism. The Executive Committee, often in conjunction with the city soviet, and the Party evaluate the fulfillment of the quarterly indices by city departments and enterprises, and they pass a resolution setting down both rewards and reprimands to the responsible agencies.

F   The city also operates under several long-range plans. First are the seven- or five-year plans for the Soviet Union as a whole. These plans

are approved with much fanfare and made into law by
the Supreme Soviet of the U.S.S.R. Leningrad, of
course, must conform to the indices laid down in
this national plan, but because the indices are
mostly for industry and agriculture, they do not
greatly affect the city government. Only in the
area of housing construction is the city directly
concerned, and here the indices are sufficiently
broad and vague so that they are not the major controlling factor. The city's own long-range plans   A
play a more decisive role. After the yearly plan,
the most important set of control indices for the
city is the two-year construction plan. Although
capital funds are allocated by the year, construction plans are drawn up for two years throughout
the Soviet Union. (Housing construction is discussed in detail in Chapter 5.)

The city's over-all development is guided by
special long-range plans which the city drafts from   ✕
time to time at the instigation of the central government. The first such long-range plan was drafted in 1939-40. The second was created in 1946-48
and updated in 1951 to cover the period to 1960.
The current plan was formulated between 1961 and
1964 and is a general twenty-year plan to 1980.
(The following section will discuss some of these
plans in detail.)

It is characteristic of all the plans relating   B
to Leningrad that they must be approved by Moscow,
and all, including the twenty-year plan, are pro-
mulgated into law and are legally binding. The
plans are approved by the executive committees and
usually their soviets at all levels of government,
from the All-Union Supreme Soviet and Council of
Ministers down to the smallest soviets and their
executive committees. Provisions of the Constitution and laws passed by the various soviets or
their presidiums are often ignored in practice or
altered by administrative fiat of the leadership
without bothering to go through the formal amending
process. Nevertheless, enacting plans into law
indicates the seriousness with which the planning
process is endowed in the Soviet Union.

At the center of planning both in the republic
and All-Union governments, the most influential organ is Gosplan, the State Planning Commission, attached to the Council of Ministers. It has a hierarchy of organs down to the local level. Although
Gosplan was constantly being reorganized under
Khrushchev, under the present leaders it has re-
turned to its more traditional form and mode of operation. It is in charge of all planning, and has
wide powers to adjust all proposed plans from below
to fit into the over-all goals set down by the
leadership. It has its own system of verification
A on the fulfillment of plans. ⌈One of the most important tasks of the Leningrad city government
and its top officials is therefore lobbying with
Gosplan officials in Moscow for desired allocations
and goals.⌋

BUDGET

Each December, the city soviet passes the budget of the city without amendments and with a minimum of discussion. The budget contains an accounting of expenditures of the previous year and proposed expenditures for the coming year. In Leningrad, it also contains the budgets for the nineteen
rayons within the city. As presented, the budget
is broken down into the broadest categories. The
soviet's approval, however, is only a matter of
form, and even the Executive Committee's prior ac-
ceptance is not crucial in the budget process. The
important hurdle is the inclusion of the budget
into the state budgets of the R.S.F.S.R. by the
Council of Ministers of the Republic. This absolute veto over the city's budget is one more way by
which Moscow exercises central control.

The major purpose of the budget--as of other
plans at the city level--is to coordinate individual plans of the city government's various bureaus
and departments with the sources of local income
and the few decisions within local discretion.
Theoretically, the city budget is also supposed to

provide coordination among all other institutions
and enterprises operating in the city, but there is
little evidence of this being done in fact.

Thus the city's primary concern in the budget,   A
as in the yearly plan, is not initiating new programs but maintaining such balances for the area as
a supply-resource balance, an income-expenditure
balance, and a fuel balance. The primary organ
assisting and directing the Executive Committee in
this coordinating process is the Ministry of Finance, which works through the city's Department of
Finance. Its primary responsibility is to see that
the city's plans are in conformity with the national budget as approved by the U.S.S.R. Council of
Ministers.

Unfortunately for the analyst, budget figures   B
for the city are extremely scarce. In recent years,
only the gross figures for income and expenditure
have been made available. Budgets are traditionally not considered a matter of concern to the public, and the details are treated as vital to the
security of the U.S.S.R. The last year that even
a limited breakdown of the budget was made available was 1962. Budget figures for selected years
through 1962 are shown in Table 10. In subsequent
years, only total income and expenditure figures
were given. There has been only a gradual increase
in both, and the basic operations covered by these
finances remain the same. (See Table 11.)

The rayon budgets are included in the city
budget. Expected expenditure and source of funds
for each rayon are shown in Table 12.

From the published discussions of the budget
and an analysis of income, it is possible to determine the following state taxes that have been assigned to Leningrad by the R.S.F.S.R. Council of
Ministers.

TABLE 10

Budget for the City of Leningrad
(1,000 rubles)

	1950	1956	1960	1962	City Budget Funds Allocated to Rayons (1962)
Income					
State enterprises	75,805	127,548	221,410	292,419	11,131
State subsidy	94,839		2,317	6,938	6,938
Local and state taxes		128,217	72,192	82,659	78,605
Turnover taxes	50,323		76,462	105,502	73,428
Other		15,796	22,532	24,854	18,896
Total*	210,624	278,427	394,904	512,372	178,998
Expenditures					
City economy	77,445	123,463	198,715	280,196	37,317
Social-cultural	119,720	135,424	184,254	216,111	159,989
Maintenance of organization		33,365	5,953	4,749	2,673
Miscellaneous	10,577	4,063	2,091	2,027	19
Total*	207,742	273,823	393,330	503,333	189,998

*No explanation is given in the original source for differences between sums of the columns and totals given.

TABLE 11

Budget Levels for the City of Leningrad, 1964-65
(in rubles)

Year	Income	Expenditure
1964	566,856,000	558,513,000
1965	561,798,000	557,197,000
1966*	624,389,000	622,361,000

*Planned

Source: Compiled by author from Biulleten
Ispolkoma lengorsoveta [Bulletin of the Executive
Committee of the Leningrad City Soviet].

TEXT ↓

Allocation to rayon budgets:

20 per cent of the lottery state bonds

25 per cent of the money lottery

100 per cent of income tax on rayon social
organizations

100 per cent of tax on bachelors and small
families

From 7 to 100 per cent of turnover and income
tax retained by rayon. (See Table 12.)

Allocation to the city budget:

12 per cent of turnover tax on bread and
liquor

5 per cent of the 3 per cent prize-winning
state bonds

TABLE 12

Planned Revenue and Expenditure for
<u>Rayons</u> of Leningrad, 1962

	Expenditure (1,000 rubles)	% of Turn-over Tax Retained	% of Income Tax Retained
Rayon			
Dzerzhinskii	8,894	4.7	18.0
Frunzenskii	9,146	1.3	7.0
Leninskii	9,340	1.6	11.0
Kalininskii	13,783	12.3	15.0
Kirovskii	11,745	22.9	11.0
Kuibishevskii	9,501	0.3	13.0
Moskovskii	16,626	2.6	19.0
Nevskii	10,953	9.4	15.0
Oktiabroskii	11,451	14.9	12.0
Petrogradskii	8,166	8.9	10.0
Smol'ninskii	11,419	25.5	16.0
Vasileostrovskii	16,759	13.5	15.0
Viborgskii	13,241	31.5	16.0
Zhdanovskii	10,382	6.8	16.0
Suburbs			
Kolpinskii	5,472	74.0	71.0
Kronshtadtskii	3,234*	100.0	100.0
Petrodvortsovskii	5,150	6.4	100.0
Pushkinskii	4,568**	100.0	100.0
Sestroretskii	7,168	100.0	100.0
Total***	189,998		

*Includes budget subsidy of 2,230,000 rubles.

**Includes budget subsidy of 3,893,000 rubles.

***No explanation is given in the original
source for differences between sums of the columns
and totals given.

Source: <u>O plane razvitiia gor. khoz. Len.</u>
[<u>Concerning the plan of development for the economy
of the city of Leningrad</u>] (Leningrad, 1962), p. 2.

⌐Therefore, there are only two areas in which   A
the city and <u>rayons</u> can increase revenue by their
own efforts: (1) They can increase the profits of
the enterprises under their control and thus increase the allocation to the budget; (2) Because
they are responsible for selling state lottery
tickets and bonds, they can increase their revenue
by making greater efforts in their sales.⌐However,   B
in respect to other sources of income such as rent,
income taxes, and other taxes, rates are set by the
central government.│By a law of October 30, 1959,
the U.S.S.R. granted the republic governments the
right to all income from enterprises subordinate to
the local soviets, thereby theoretically freeing
large amounts of local revenue. Republic governments were then supposed to allocate a portion or
all of these profits to local government. In
practice, however, All-Union control did not cease,
and the very powerful U.S.S.R. Ministry of Finance
continued to supervise and curtail the distribution
of these profits. The Finance Ministry has been
openly criticized for its obstructionism but apparently to little avail.

⌐Expenditures covered by the budget do not in- C ✕
clude operations of the city-owned enterprises.
Most city enterprises are set up as separate accounting and legal entities under Soviet law and
have separate budgets. Merely a portion of their
profits appear in the city's budget under income.
Although these enterprises have separate budgets,
they are included in the yearly production plan for
the city.│

⌐Similarly, capital expenditures, except for   D
some minor items, are not included in the city budget. For example, in 1962 the plan for new construction provided for an expenditure of 248.7 million rubles, of which only 26.1 million rubles were
to come from the city budget. The remaining amount
was centrally allocated through the state plan for
construction of the R.S.F.S.R. The limited capital
funds that are included in the city's budget are
used primarily for extensions of such public services as water, sewage, and transportation lines.

Capital expenditures for all units of government and most of the economy are closely controlled
from the center by the All-Union Council of Ministers
through the republic governments. As will be discussed in Chapter 5, capital construction in particular has become increasingly centralized both in allocation and execution. Local governments, however,
can accumulate limited amounts of capital from
profits, particularly unplanned profits, certain
other collections, and bonuses. These they can use
for the construction of housing, rest homes, and
recreational facilities.

YEARLY AND QUARTERLY PLANS

Primary responsibility is placed on the Planning Commission of the Executive Committee for
drafting the yearly and quarterly plans, which are
more comprehensive plans than the budget. In fact,
the budget is really only one part of the yearly
plan. The importance of the Planning Commission is
indicated by the fact that one of the vice-chairmen
of the Presidium is also head of the commission.
A As mentioned previously, not all of the departments
of the local government are included directly in
the city's plan. For example, education, which has
B its own budget, is excluded. The subdivisions of
the city-planning commission give some indication
of the competence of the city in drafting plans.
These subdivisions include the following: (1) com-
posite plans; (2) finance and costs; (3) prices;
(4) transport and communications; (5) housing construction; (6) housing economy; (7) communal economy; (8) enlightenment, culture, and welfare;
(9) daily services; (10) trade and general provisions; (11) industry; (12) planning work cadres;
(13) contract organizations; (14) capital outlay
and project work for the city's economy; (15) material balance; and (16) capital construction control.

C   In drawing up the preliminary plan, the commission works with each rayon's planning commission
and with planning groups and chiefs of the various

city departments. The Party and trade unions also
have sections interested in the planning process,
but it is not known how active they are.   The final
draft plan is brought together by the Planning Commission, the Presidium, and top Party officials.
These organs in turn negotiate the final plan with
the State Planning Commision (Gosplan) and the
R.S.F.S.R. Council of Ministers.   The City Planning
Commission is also responsible to the State Planning Commission for techniques of planning and for
reporting on the plan's fulfillment.

The Finance Department and the State Bank keep
close watch on the plan's financial aspects.   The
State Bank, for example, reviews financing and the
technical form of the plan and must approve as con-
forming to the plan all city transactions involving
more than 50 rubles.   Trade unions and the Party
also take part in the planning and assume a general
responsibility for seeing that the city administration fulfills the plan.⌐

⌐The yearly plan provides indices for total   A
production, productivity, money turnover, salary
funds, and profits for each of the departments and
enterprises under the city and for the city as a
whole.⌐ Some over-all goals set by the plan for
1962 demonstrate the scope of this process.   For
example, public-service goals included provision
for 572.6 million cubic meters of water and 2.7
billion cubic meters of gas, service for 51 million
customers in the public baths, washing of 18,800
tons of clothes; repairing 635,000 square meters of
roads; public transportation for 1.9 billion passengers, 65.9 million movie admissions, and 2.38
million theater admissions.   Additionally, it
planned to operate 447,920 general school pupil-
places, 64,860 nursery school pupil-places, 36,115
places in creches; and 31,330 hospital beds.   Construction goals called for 34 miles of new water
lines; 31 miles of new sewage lines; 62 miles of
new gas lines; 500,000 square meters of new asphalt
roads; and installation of gas in 41,000 apartments.

The output goal of 894.9 million rubles of
production was set for enterprises subordinate to
the city. Included in this were 241 million rubles
from local industries; 153.9 million rubles from
light industries; and 142.4 million rubles from
bread industries.

Of the 73.5 million rubles expected from
daily-services output, 44.2 million rubles was the
goal for the Department of Daily Services, and 12.9
million rubles was the output goal for the Department of Daily-Services Enterprises. The Department
of Trade had a goal of 10.3 million rubles, and the
output goal for the television reception system was
2.9 million rubles.

Trade and turnover of general provisions were
planned at 2.7 billion rubles. Productivity in the
city's industries was to increase 4.8 per cent in
1962. The salary role of the city in its industries, construction, trade organizations, and departments was set at 365,900 workers with a salary
fund of 369 million rubles.

The planning figures represent an over-all annual increase of services and production from 5 to
15 per cent. Such an increase is significant, giv-
en the limited resources and low priority of local
government. Therefore, it is not unusual for the
city and its rayons to fail to meet the plan in
several categories. For example, eleven of the
fourteen rayons in the city failed to meet their
plan targets for 1965. Nevertheless, over the decade that began with the decision to increase consumers goods after the death of Stalin, and with
the housing construction program initiated in the
late 1950's, continuous expansion of urban services
has become a built-in attribute of the local government structure. Thus, at least one-sixth of the
city's working force and many of the departmental
offices are permanently engaged in developing new
services. In the short run, it is not likely that
this balance will be altered, because of the com-
mitment of the present leadership to continue to

improve living standards, particularly housing.
However, if the present trend of decreasing immigration into the city of Leningrad continues, the
rate of expansion for new facilities will certainly
decline.

⌐ In conclusion, the annual budget and planning   A
process provides another example of how the city
has been made subordinate to central authorities
and also shows the broad scope of the city's activities in the local economy. The city employs almost one-quarter of the working population within
it.   Thus, even though the city government may not
have an important policy-making and financial role
in its own development, it is an economic unit of
tremendous size, and the Executive Committee and
departments manage about three-quarters of the
economy's consumer sector in the Leningrad area.⌐

THE TWO-YEAR CONSTRUCTION PLAN

⌐ A "title list" of new buildings and other   B
large construction projects such as water purification plants is drawn up for the city on the basis
of a two-year period. The central agency for this
plan at the local level is the Architect-Planning
Department. In general, it works with a lead time
of almost two years, so that in 1965 it was working
on the 1967-68 plan. The other main participants
in this planning at the local level are the City
Planning Commission, the Presidium, the chiefs and
planning sections of the Construction Department
and Construction Material Department, and the State
Construction Bank (Stroibank). ⌐ The local Construc-   C
tion Department, Construction Materials Department,
and the Construction Bank are branches of central
ministries or commissions, as is the Architect-
Planning Department. Because capital construction
was completely centralized in 1962, the final draft
and approval of the city's construction plan comes
from Gosplan and the U.S.S.R. Ministry of Construction, through Gosplan and the R.S.F.S.R. Ministry
of Construction. ⌐

A   ⌜The actual construction is done by contract
between a trust or <u>combinat</u>[1] subordinate to the
Department of Capital Construction attached to the
executive committee of the city soviet and the re-
ceiving party, which in the case of housing is
B   primarily the city. (See Chapter 5.)⌝ Major responsibility for verifying fulfillment of the construction plan rests with Gosplan, with the Construction Bank (which must approve all payments on
the basis of the proper fulfillment of tasks), and
with the recipient of the construction (such as the
city).[2] The Party and trade unions also have an
over-all responsibility for checking performance.
In spite of the number of agencies involved, the
Soviets admit that verifying operations are faulty.
Frequent articles appear in the press pointing out
how the city and other agencies fail to properly
supervise housing under construction and only in-
spect halfheartedly when the building is completed,
often too late to rectify errors.⌟

Part of the capital construction plan is the
capital repair program. In 1962, it amounted to
100.6 million rubles, about one-quarter of the total capital expenditure, of which 54 million rubles
C   was to repair housing. ⌜As will be discussed in
Chapter 5, capital repair, unlike new construction,
is closely integrated into the city's economy.
For example, the Department of Capital Repairs reports directly to the city, and part of the funds
for capital repairs comes from the amortization cost
charged to renters, particularly to enterprises
renting nonresidential space in city buildings.⌟

LONG-RANGE PLANNING

The long-range plan currently valid for Leningrad was drafted by the Architect-Planning Department and completed in 1964. It was subsequently
approved by the Executive Committee, and reviewed
by experts in the State Economic Committee and
State Construction Committee, before it was given
its final approval by the U.S.S.R. Council of Ministers.

Earlier, general plans had established the idea of a greenbelt around the city. Since the suburban area has had meager development and is made up of two-thirds forest and one-fourth agricultural, it was relatively easy to set up a greenbelt. This forest park around the city is 15.30 kilometers (9.5 miles) from the city's center and includes an area of 280,000 hectares (691,600 acres). The current plan provides that 230,000 hectares (568,100 acres) will be maintained in their natural state with a limited number of roads and services. On the remaining 50,000 hectares (123,500 acres), the city will construct roads and extensive public services. The Executive Committee has ordered 2,000 hectares (4,940 acres) of the forest park to be developed each year.

When the Architect-Planning Department first began its general plan in 1962, it was thought that the population in greater Leningrad, which includes both the urban and rural rayons, would increase 2 million by 1972 and an additional 1.2 million by 1980. The population in the older urban rayons was planned at about 3 million; some 2.5 million were to be relocated in new cities and 800,000 in the countryside. With this dispersal, the number of commuters to the city was expected to increase to 700,000. But as the plan actually emerged in 1964, the concept of a vast population center with several new towns around the city was dropped. The planners no longer thought in terms of an over-all population of more than 6 million for the Leningrad area, as the population trend of recent years has shown that this figure was unrealistic. In 1959, the population increase for Leningrad and its suburbs was about 60,000 a year and seemed to be increasing, but in the next four years, the rate declined to less than 30,000 a year and continues to decrease. (See Table 13.) As a result, no new estimates have been made in planning for greater Leningrad, but the city proper will be stabilized at a level of about 3.3 million up through 1980. This means that the population will gradually be moved out of the heart of the city, and new living

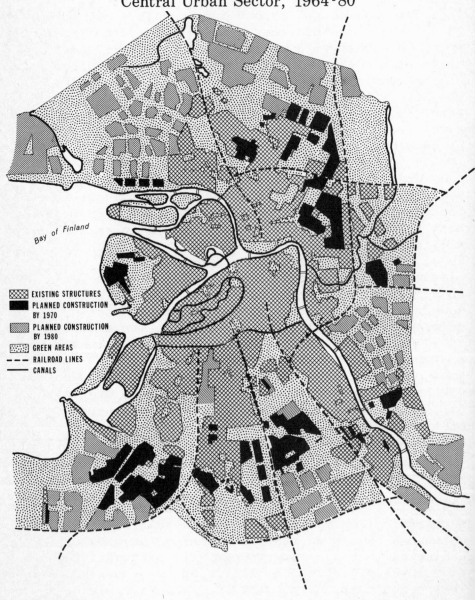

Map 2

Long-Range Construction Plans for Leningrad's
Central Urban Sector, 1964-80

Bay of Finland

EXISTING STRUCTURES
PLANNED CONSTRUCTION BY 1970
PLANNED CONSTRUCTION BY 1980
GREEN AREAS
RAILROAD LINES
CANALS

rayons of 25,000 to 50,000 persons will be developed
on the edges of the city. These will become new
trade and cultural centers. The question of new
satellite cities is left open and will depend on
whether increased immigration and population growth
might push the city beyond its 3.3 million ceiling,
but in 1968 none were planned, because of the great
expense and the uncertain and falling rate of population growth.

TABLE 13

Estimated Annual Population Increases in
Leading Cities of the Soviet Union
(in 1,000's)

	Greater Leningrad	Leningrad Proper	Moscow Proper	Kiev	Gorky
1959	62	48	99	35	31
1960	62	49	100	35	30
1961	53	39	54	34	22
1962	54	44	55	40	17
1963	55	38	36	40	16
1964	34	21	31	40	19
1965	24	22*	28	35	15

*Beginning in 1965, a slightly larger terri-
torial base was used.

Source: Compiled by author.

Construction in the city through 1980 will be
considerable. For the purpose of long-range planning and construction, the city has been divided
into fourteen large planning areas of about 200,000
to 300,000 people. The old factories in the city

will be remodeled, and all new factories will be moved to industrial zones outside the city. Between 1964 and 1980, in the urban rayons the city expects to build 29 million square meters of housing space (10 million square meters in 1964-70, and 19 million[3] in 1971-80). This will raise the living space to 12.5 square meters per person in 1975 and to 15 square meters per person in 1980. Expected increases for some of the public services are shown in Table 14 and Table 15.

The main emphasis on developing new recreational areas will be along the seacoast: five miles along the south coast, seven miles in the city, and four miles along the north coast.

The Architect-Planning Office, in presenting the plan in 1964, stressed that the plan was not static and was in a constant process of being revised. Almost monthly, the periodical, Stroitelstvo i arkhitektura Leningrada [Construction and Architecture in Leningrad], organ of the Executive Committee and Architect-Planning Department, publishes an article containing new or modified development projects for some part of the city, although not all of these projects receive final approval for inclusion in the general plan.

Fulfillment or nonfulfillment of long-range plans is really out of the city's control and depends on the priorities that the national leaders assign in allocating capital funds, their willingness to support the continued growth of Leningrad, and the manner of their support. Individual ministries also affect the plan, and they have considerable power in determining where new enterprises will be constructed. In fact, this was a major reason why the population restrictions on Leningrad before 1959 did not work. Ministries continued building new enterprises and expanding old ones in Leningrad to take advantage of established services and skilled manpower, thereby creating pressures for more workers. The city has little control over building or expansion of basic industrial facilities

in its area, except that it does have considerable
voice as to the exact location of a new plant or
building within the city.

TABLE 14

Planned Output of Electricity in the
City of Leningrad, 1960-80

Year	Kilowatt Hours (in millions)
1960	1.17
1970	2.83
1980	7.75

Source: Stroitelstvo i arkhitektura Leningrada
[Construction and Architecture in Leningrad], No. 6
(1964).

TABLE 15

Planned Volume of Passenger Transportation
in the City of Leningrad, 1962-80

Mode of Transportation	1962		1970		1980	
	Passengers (in millions)	Per Cent	Passengers (in millions)	Per Cent	Passengers (in millions)	Per Cent
Metro	149	8.1	480	20.5	900	32.1
Bus	523	28.3	720	30.5	800	28.5
Trolley bus	237	12.8	340	14.5	550	19.7
Tram	939	50.8	800	34.5	550	19.7
Total	1,848	100.0	2,340	100.0	2,800	100.0

Source: Stroitelstvo i arkhitektura Leningrada
[Construction and Architecture in Leningrad], No. 6
(1964).

CONCLUSION

Over the years, the city of Leningrad has developed an impressive array of short range and long
range plans. The twenty-year plan is particularly
significant because it projects the smooth and careful expansion of the city and all its surrounding
A area to 1980. ⌈And because public authority is so
broad and the pressure of private entrepreneurs is
lacking, the city would seem to be in a good posi-
B tion to operationalize the plan. ⌈But such an op-
timistic view of planning in Leningrad is deceptive.

The Soviet planning system in general has come
under increasing criticism. As the economy becomes
more complex, it has become increasingly difficult
to coordinate the intricacies of the plan. Increased manpower and the introduction of computers
has not been enough. Furthermore, the planning
system provides no real measure of efficiency or of
optimum use of resources. Finally, the planning
indexes, except for the most crude one of total
C output, are largely unenforceable. ⌈In addition to
these general problems of planning in the Soviet
Union, local governments have special problems.
The regime has persistently left local governments
short of funds, and when some part of the country's
plan must be sacrificed local industries and services are one of the first areas to be cut. ²All
plans of local government are forever subject to
the approval and capriciousness of central authorities. Finally, ³cities often find it difficult to
coordinate their plans with the numerous agencies
and factories of the central ministries operating
in the area. The next two chapters discuss some of
these problems in Leningrad and how several of the
city's services and housing are administered and
their plans operationalized.

NOTES TO CHAPTER 3

1. <u>Combinats</u> or trusts are enterprises or other organizations that provide goods and services and are in themselves financially and legally responsible for their operations. They are similar to government corporations in the West, but their independence in decision-making has usually been more restricted.

2. Current planning indices for construction are primarily volume of construction assembly work at estimated prices; sum of wages paid as per cent of work volume; and time span for completions.

3. More recent discussions mention a figure of 18 million square meters.

CHAPTER **4** SELECTED

SERVICES

MINISTERIAL AND LOCAL CONTROL

As stated in Chapter 2, the various public and communal services and local industries which number among the city's departments and are organized under the city's Executive Committee, are at the same time under the control of a republic or union-republic ministry. They are subordinate to the following ministries of the R.S.F.S.R.: the Union Republic Ministries of Welfare, Culture, Meat and Milk Industries, Food Production Industries, Trade and Finance; and the Republic Ministries of Communal Economy, Consumer Services, Local Industries, Public Education, Social Security, Fuel Industries and Bread Industries.

The amount of discretion and administrative decision-making permitted to the city authorities A varies greatly. ⌈In the case of electricity, the city plays a minor role, merely overseeing distribution to the population. The role of the Finance Department as part of the city government is even more tenuous. It is a department intimately bound up in all the activities of local government but is not subject to the Executive Committee's control. In fact, in many respects it controls the activities of the Executive Committee. At the other extreme, the city operates the Sewage and Water Department with a minimum of interference except for B major capital expenditures and basic rates.⌋ ⌈In some matters (such as gas supplies) the city's

jurisdiction seems to be declining, while in others
(such as local police) it seems to be increasing.
In no area is the local government completely free   A
from some central surveillance, but in general there
is more local discretion over those departments not
subject to direct ministerial subordination.

One of the major tasks of the ministries in
setting the policies of the various services for
local government is to conduct research and set
standards or norms. Attached to the ministries are
various research institutes and even an academy.
Leningrad, the second city of the U.S.S.R. (in a
differently designated climatic zone[1] from Moscow)
and an educational center, has several branch research institutes of central ministries. For example, the Academy of Communal Economy in Moscow
has an affiliated institute in Leningrad. Although
these institutes are responsible only to Moscow,
they work closely with local departments and give
Leningrad a special status. About one-quarter of
the studies on local government and economy come
out of the Leningrad institutes and use Leningrad
as a case study.

A major source of communicating new techniques
and ideas to local city governments is the monthly
Zhilishchno-kommunalnoe khoziaestvo [Living-Communal
Economy], published by the Ministry of Communal
Economy. It contains highly technical articles on
new methods of management and maintenance but occasionally also has articles and editorials discussing current problems. Its editorials are, however,
not as critical of the system as are many in the
architectural journals.

For the outside analyst, it is difficult to
fathom the lines of responsibility and communica-
tion within the local government and with the central authorities. The literature and the Soviet
laws and regulations setting up the legal framework
give only the barest skeleton. For example, the
descriptions of the various departments of local
government in the Executive Committee orders

establishing them often do not even include their
formal functions. It is impossible from available
written materials to distinguish between the roles
and duties of the Department of Capital Construction and the Department of Housing and Civil and
Industrial Construction, or between the Internal
Affairs Department and the General Affairs Depart-
A ment. [It is possible to clarify some details
through interviews, but the relationships and functions are unstable. The pattern of authority,
which depends to a large extent on the personal position of the department head and the priorities
and interests of the city's leadership, the Party,
and the central government is forever changing.
The system can be considered a model of authoritarian government with an overlay of formal legal institutions. The legal institutions, however, are
sufficiently vague so that they do not interfere
with the basic characteristic of the authoritarian
regime, which includes the ability of the leadership to change at will the direction, form, and
purpose of institutions and groups. As we have
seen, in the Soviet Union these changes have pur-
posely been made frequently to keep the system
flexible and responsible to the wishes of the
leaders.

In conclusion, any description of the operation of the various services in the city must be
tentative and incomplete, giving only a general
impression of their structure and functions and a
history of their development.

WATER AND SEWERAGE

Leningrad has an abundance of fresh water from
the Neva River and Lake Ladoga, only about nineteen
miles away. In the early days of Saint Petersburg,
canals were dug from the Neva to various parts of
the city, and from them water was piped or carried
by wagon to the consumers. In the first half of
the nineteenth century, small private pumping stations were created, but they were unable to supply

the needs of the rapidly growing city. In 1858,
the first large company for pumping water from the
Neva was created to furnish water to the central
part of the city. It began operating in 1863.
Soon, other large companies were formed. The first
filtration plant was constructed in 1887-89; it was
followed by others, but by 1913, less than two-
thirds of the water supply was filtered and purified. In 1913, the city duma [assembly] adopted a
major project to bring water directly from Lake
Ladoga to the city, but the project was abandoned
during the war and the Revolution.

By the time of the Revolution, there were two
main pumping stations and two substations with inadequate purification systems, all under the city
government. With the Revolution, efforts to purify
the water almost ceased, and a new system of purification at one of the main stations was started in
1927 and completed in 1932. In the mid-1930's, the
second large station was rebuilt, and a third major
pumping station was added, each with a purification
system. The plan to tap Lake Ladoga was then renewed, but again war interrupted execution. During
the siege of World War II, the water did not stop
flowing although many of the pipes froze in the
winter of 1941-42. Today, there are three major
pumping stations and seven substations providing
filtered and purified water from the Neva, but the
project to pump water directly from Lake Ladoga has
still not been realized and seems to have been permanently dropped. The average per capita consumption had risen from 34.3 gallons in 1917 to 101.7
gallons in 1956. The consumption of water in the
city's urban rayons is about 580 million cubic
meters per year. The general plan calls for another major pumping station on the Neva by 1980.
There has never been a serious shortage of water,
and until recently no efforts have been made to
limit consumption. Water has not been metered, but
starting in 1965 the city began to install water
meters. However, only 200 were scheduled for installation in 1965.

The first sewage pipes conducting waste to the
canals and rivers from Saint Petersburg were begun
in 1770. By 1834, there were 59 miles of sewage
pipes (Paris in 1830 had only 28 miles), and by
1917 there were 301 miles, covering 60 per cent of
the streets. However, 220 miles of the system had
only wooden lines.

The growing pollution of the canals and rivers
brought about by the city's rapid growth in the
latter half of the nineteenth century, created an
acute need for some type of sewage disposal. From
1884 to 1911, some 65 projects for sewage disposal
were considered, and a world contest for a solution
was held in 1900. All plans were rejected in the
end. Finally, in 1913, the city parliament approved an over-all system similar to that suggested
by an Englishman, Lindley, in 1884. The city was
divided into 29 districts, each with a pumping station. The pumping stations were to pump the sewage
10 miles outside the city, process and return the
water to the Neva. World War I and the Revolution
interrupted the plan. In 1925, a modified plan was
adopted, dividing Leningrad into 4 basins, each
with its own disposal system. The first plant,
covering the center of the city, was completed in
1930. The second, covering Vasilli Island, was
completed in 1935. The other two soon followed.
A general plan for sewage disposal in the city's
new areas in the south and east was adopted in 1940
but was interrupted by the war. A revised general
plan was adopted by the city soviet in 1947 and
approved by the various central ministries in 1949-
51, by the State Committee for Construction in 1952
and by the Council of Ministers of the U.S.S.R. in
1953. There have been some additional revisions of
the plan with the development of new areas. An
average of 25 to 31 miles of sewage lines have been
added to the system each year.

A single Department of Water and Sewage has
operated both services since World War II. It has
no rayon subdepartments, and the housing bureaus
collect the per capita charges for water and sewage

from the population. It has been one of the most
stable and autonomously functioning departments of
the city. Since 1948, there have been only two
heads of the department, both serving long terms.
Except for setting rates and norms and providing
for major capital expenditures, Moscow permits the
city to operate its own water and sewage system and
provide for minor capital outlays. For these expenditures, the department is self-sufficient, operating largely on the fees collected.

WATER POLLUTION

In recent years, the major source of water
pollution has been industry. Most industries are
not connected with the city sewage system but have
their own system or dump sewage directly into the
river or canals. On Vasilli Island and in the
Leninskii Rayon in the 1950's, special systems were
constructed to dispose of industrial waste. But in
other parts of the city, large plants were made responsible for their own waste-disposal systems.
This has created a major source of conflict between
the city and those industries under centralized
ministries. Normally, conflicts between departments of government in the Soviet Union are settled
quietly, beyond the public eye. But in this case,
the powerful industries and centralized ministries
--interested in economizing on scarce capital and
resources--persistently ignored the city's pleas.
As a result, in a resolution on March 6, 1961, with
some encouragement from the republic authorities,
the city took the unusual step of publicizing their
dispute with these industries and publicly appeal-
ing for a solution. Apparently many individual
plant managers were sympathetic, but their ministries refused to allocate funds for building treatment systems. Still not satisfied, the Executive
Committee on April 17, 1961, passed a resolution
turning over names of directors who still refused
compliance to the procurator for criminal prosecu-
tion.[2] As a result, some remedial actions must
have been taken, because the most recent references

to this problem in the Executive Committee's resolutions indicate that although water pollution by
industry has not been entirely eliminated, there
has been some improvement. For example, in a resolution on July 11, 1964, 118 plants had taken action to construct water purification systems for
their wastes, and an additional 102 enterprises had
agreed to take action by 1967. But at the same
time, in a resolution on July 10, 1964, the Executive Committee publicly complained that industries
had failed to clear and beautify their river and
canal banks.

GAS SUPPLY

The first production of gas for lighting began
in Saint Petersburg in 1835. By the end of the
nineteenth century, there were five factories producing about 30 million cubic meters per year. By
the time of the Revolution, gas consumption had
fallen by about 50 per cent, as electricity re-
placed gas for lighting streets and homes, but gas
was becoming increasingly important as a fuel
source for cooking and heating. The coal shortage
during the civil war brought an end to the production of gas in March, 1920. Gas production was not
resumed until 1935, only to be halted again in 1941
as a result of the Nazi bombardment of the city.
Production did not begin again until 1946. By a
decision of the U.S.S.R. Council of Ministers on
June 10, 1945, not only was gas production to be
restored, but construction was planned for three
new factories capable of producing 2.8 billion cubic meters; 24 substations were to be restored
and/or constructed; and 620 miles of street lines
were to be laid. This general plan was later modified by the introduction of natural gas. Until
about 1956, and during the period of major reconstruction and construction of gas facilities, there
was a separate Department of Construction of Gas
Works in addition to the general operating department (Department of Gas Economy).[3] By 1964, 95 per
cent of all housing was supplied with gas; in 1961,

gas lines had been extended to the two largest satellite cities of Pushkin and Kolpino. Gas consumption increased from 25.3 million cubic meters in
1946 to 779 million cubic meters in 1958. Most of
the gas produced in the city (70-80 per cent) was
used directly by the population and local economy,
and only a small part was used by industry. Then,
during 1959-60, natural gas from the Ukraine was
piped to Leningrad and industry became almost immediately the prime user. By 1963, gas consumption
had increased to 3.45 billion cubic meters, of
which industry consumed 73 per cent. The result
has been a major shift in the city's fuel balance,
as shown by Table 16. Table 17 indicates that the
major consumer of all fuels is industry.

TABLE 16

Fuel Balance in Leningrad and Suburbs

	1958		1960		1965 (Planned)	
	1,000 Tons	Per Cent	1,000 Tons	Per Cent	1,000 Tons	Per Cent
Coal	5,010	65.2	4,713	50.9	1,200	11.5
Oil shales	587	7.7	587	6.3	580	5.6
Peat	248	3.2	622	6.7	330	3.2
Firewood	471	6.2	366	4.0	300	2.9
Petroleum	1,222	15.9	1,475	15.9	3,300	31.7
Natural gas			1,247	13.4	4,450	42.8
Other	144	1.8	258	2.8	340	2.3
Total	7,682	100.0	9,268	100.0	10,500	100.0

Source: Leningradskaia gor. konferentsiia po
okhrane atmosfernovo vozdukha [Leningrad City Conference on the Prevention of Atmospheric Pollution]
(Leningrad, 1963), pp. 21-24.

TABLE 17

Fuel Consumption According to Use in
Leningrad and Suburbs, 1960

Consumer	Tons of Fuel	Per Cent
Industry	6,495,000	70.1
Construction	231,000	2.3
Transport	960,000	10.4
Housing	964,000	10.4
Other	618,000	6.6
Total	9,268,000	99.8

Source: Leningradskaia gor. konferentsiia po
okhrane atmosfernovo vozdukha [Leningrad City Conference on the Prevention of Atmospheric Pollution]
(Leningrad, 1963), pp. 21-24.

Prior to the changeover to natural gas, administration of the gas-producing industries and of
distribution was primarily the city's responsibility. But with the advent of natural gas and the
conversion to the new fuel by many industries, the
center of administration has shifted to the Fuel
Industries Ministry at the republic level.

Because of the unavailability and cost of meters, the city does not meter the gas used by individual consumers but charges 30 kopecks [33 cents
per person per month.

AIR POLLUTION

Although the major reason for the shift to
natural gas was economic, the growing problem of
air pollution was also a factor. A study made of

two boarding schools (one with a pollution level of
.63 milligrams of hydrocarbons per cubic meter and
the other with a pollution level of only .20 milligrams), showed that the respiratory diseases in the
former were 1.5 to 2.4 times those in the latter,
depending on the type of infection. The average
pollution in Leningrad in 1958 was .66 milligrams
per cubic meter but varied with season and location.
In some areas it reached as high as 3.93 milligrams
per cubic meter.[4]

Increasingly, the Executive Committee and the
Presidium have been putting pressure on industry to
reduce its air pollution by installing filter systems or by using natural gas. For example, in 1962,
15 large enterprises installed filters, and 25 enterprises adopted natural gas. The city is switch-
ing to gas as a fuel for its boiler systems for
central heating. In 1958, of 140 regional boilers,
only two were using natural gas; in 1962, of 253
regional boilers, only 85 did not use natural gas.[5]
The result is that the average level of dirt from
the air declined from 48 grams per square meter in
1959 to 37 grams in 1962.

While the problem of air pollution by industries is being solved, the amount of air pollution
from trucks and automobiles has increased rapidly
in Leningrad with the expansion of auto traffic by
4-5 per cent a year. But beyond some pious resolutions that something should be done, the city has
made no concrete efforts in this area.

PUBLIC TRANSPORTATION

In 1917, the only public transportation operated by the city was 724 tram cars that carried
241.6 million passengers a year. By 1919, the number of passengers had fallen to 151.3 million; by
1921, there were only 227 tram cars left in service.
During the early 1920's, when public transportation
was made free to the public, the system became
overburdened and lacked funds to rebuild cars and

lines. Thus, not until 1928 were the tram lines
and cars restored to their 1917 level. At the same
time, however, they were carrying twice as much
traffic (510.6 million passengers). In the 1930's,
bus lines and then trolley-bus lines were added,
increasing the total passenger traffic to 1.431
billion passengers a year by 1939. Then, at the
end of 1955, the first subway line of seven miles
was opened. Passenger traffic in the city in 1962
is shown in Table 15.

About 93 miles of bus lines are added each
year to connect new residential areas to the city.
This is necessary because few residents in Leningrad own private transportation. The subway lines
are also being extended. Two lines were opened in
1965, and a third line was scheduled for 1967.
Eventually a whole network of subways is planned ,
including an outer ring to connect all of them. By
1990, Leningrad plans to have 73 miles of subway.[6]
It is calculated that subways will carry one-third
of the passenger traffic in the future.

The fare for public transportation is nominal:
3 kopecks for trams, 4 kopecks for trolley buses,
and 5 kopecks for buses and subways. In spite of
minimal fares, however, the services do not run at
a loss. One reason is the relatively low wages of
the workers, ranging from 60 to 120 rubles per
month. Furthermore, the number of workers recently
was reduced by dispensing with most of the conductors and allowing passengers to pay on their own.
Ticket boxes are placed in the front and back of
the conveyance, and each passenger drops in his
fare and tears off a ticket. It is primarily the
responsibility of the other passengers to see that
it is done honestly, although there are also roving
public inspectors who occasionally check tickets.
Currently, 59 per cent of the vehicles (except the
subway) are without conductors. A second reason,
and the most important for their financial success,
is that the services are used to capacity, and in
fact are notoriously overcrowded even at off-hours.

RETAIL TRADE

In 1931, all private trade outlets in Leningrad were abolished by law; in 1935, cooperative trade in the city was liquidated and turned over to the state trading system. Cooperative trade, however, has continued to operate in the rural areas around the city. In addition to local trade trusts, which were organized under the departments for food and for manufactured goods of the city soviet, various ministries established their own system of stores. The result was that by the beginning of World War II there were 146 different and separate trade organizations in Leningrad. The Executive Committee of the city was supposed to coordinate the system but remained in fact powerless to do so. In the postwar period, the trade system was gradually reorganized, and a large part of retail trade was brought under the city's direct administration, with over-all prices and policies set by the Union-Republic Ministry of Trade in Moscow. The ministry also maintains a corps of inspectors to check on the quality of goods and services. Leningrad is fortunate in that 88 per cent of the manufactured goods and 90 per cent of the food products sold in the city are retailed in this way, through city-administered trade organizations (torgov). In most cities of the U.S.S.R. there is much less control over trade.

In Leningrad, the city trade organizations have a volume of about 3 billion rubles a year, and the rate increases at about 4 per cent a year. Also under the Department of Daily Consumer Services attached to the Executive Committee, the city operates retail services for the population amounting to about 75 million rubles a year. These include various repair services, laundries, barbers, beauty parlors, public baths, and city hotels (12 of 37 in the city).

The organization of local trade administration within Leningrad has gone through several changes since the war. The basic unit is the trade organization (torgov), which operates retail stores for a

given type of commodity. Examples of such organiza
tions dealing with manufactured goods include:
Lenodezhda (Clothing), Lenkhoztorg (Household
Goods), Lenobuv'torg (Shoes), Mebel'torg (Furniture
Lengalantereitorg (Haberdasheries), Lensporttorg
(Sporting Goods), Lenelektrostroitorg (Electrical
Goods), and Lentrikotazhtorg (Knitted Goods).

In the immediate postwar period, trade organizations were grouped into three departments--for
manufactured goods, for public eating establish-
ments, and for fish and produce. In 1953, they
were combined into a single Department of Trade.
During the brief supremacy of Malenkov's policy of
priority for consumer's goods in the mid-1950's,
there was a proliferation of four additional departments dealing with trade and food stuffs, but
subsequently a single Department of Trade was restored. Then, in 1965, this department was divided
in two: the Department of Trade, and the Chief Department for General Food Supplies.

Certain ministries still maintain their own
trade organizations in Leningrad. The Ministry of
Health controls the pharmacies in the city; the
State Committee for the Press operates most of the
book stores; and the Ministry of Communications
operates the kiosks near and in the railway station

The only legally operated private trade is con
ducted through the commission stores (secondhand
stores) and the collective farm markets. Both are
operated by the city through the rayons. Each
rayon maintains a collective farm market where the
collective farms (kolkhoz) and the individual collective farmers from their private plots can bring
their produce to sell directly to the population.[7]
Farmers must pay a small fee for the use of a stall
in the market. These collective farm markets play
an important role in the over-all trade system.
For the U.S.S.R. as a whole, this trade represents
about 12 per cent of the total trade volume and
about 50 per cent of the trade in fruits and
vegetables.

THE MILITIA

As part of the coercive apparatus of the state, the militia under Stalin was rigidly controlled from the center and was not even represented on the Executive Committee. The militia is still under the central direction of the Department of Militia in the Union-Republic Ministry of Public Order, but in recent years increasing numbers of cooperative arrangements with the city have developed. Beginning in 1956, a Chief Department of Security was created under the Executive Committee, and the militia became a major subdivision of this department. The militia, furthermore, has branch offices in each rayon. It is budgeted locally. The organization of the druzhini (citizens' groups to maintain public order) and comradely courts in the late 1950's was another step in developing closer relations between the city and the militia.[8] The militia refer certain types of cases to the comradely courts, particularly those involving disorderly conduct, and the druzhini are in effect auxiliary militiamen helping to keep order in the evenings and on holidays. At the same time, the head of the militia or his representative is included on most of the coordinating subcommittees of the Executive Committee.

A survey of the resolutions of the Executive Committee reveals that in the 1950's matters dealing with the militia were omitted from the agenda of the Executive Committee and local soviets, but in the 1960's, in certain limited areas, the Executive Committee passed resolutions dealing with police matters. An example of the present relationship is the use made by the local militia of the Executive Committee as a lobbyist in Moscow. The local militia have taken to complaining to the city that they are not only undermanned but do not have proper facilities, especially communications equipment. In response, the Executive Committee and local press publicized the shortage and pressured Moscow for larger budget allocations and equipment.

The reason for greater local participation in

police matters is due not only to a general relaxation of central control and use of coercion, but it
also reflects a concern for the increase in crime
and general lawlessness, particularly among the
youth. In recent years, there have been several
resolutions drawing attention to the problem and
criticizing laxness of the militia and procurator
in prosecuting criminals. For example, the resolution of the Leningrad Soviet on June 15, 1961,
stated that in 1960 more than 40 per cent of the
approved applications for bail by criminals were
unfounded and that this had increased to 50 per
cent during the first quarter of 1961.[9] The city
and the central government, in an effort to check
growing delinquency, have increased the powers of
the militia and mobilized local resources to back
the militia. The power of the militia to fine for
misdemeanors has been restored. A militiaman can
levy a fine of 1 ruble on the spot, and a militia
administrative commission can fine up to 10 rubles
and in some cases 50 rubles with the approval of
the local soviet. The curfew hours for youth under
the age of eighteen of 9:00 P.M. in the winter and
10:00 P.M. in summer and the ban on their consumption or purchase of beer and tobacco are being more
strictly enforced. The local druzhini and comradely courts were also designed to supplement the power and the limited resources of the militia for
purposes of controlling disorderly conduct but not
to apprehend criminals.

More important have been professional and administrative auxiliary organs. At the instigation
of the central government, the Executive Committee
appointed a collegium to improve the work and science of public security. It is chaired by the head
of the Security Department and has seven members
from departments dealing in security matters. The
Executive Committee also appointed a high-level
coordinating committee on youth affairs, led by a
vice-chairman of the Executive Committee and including as members the heads of those departments
in the city, Party, and trade unions dealing with
youth. The vice-chairman is the head of the

Department of Education, and also on the committee
are representatives of the militia, the Department
of Social Security, the Komsomols, the Department
of Security, the Department of Culture, the Department of Welfare, and various _rayon_ authorities.
Its work is designed to be preventative by planning
controls and activities to keep the youth well oc-
cupied. One of the basic problems is that Soviet
youth have become increasingly bored with the inef-
fectual, highly propagandistic, recreational activities organized by the Komsomols and trade unions.

FIRE PREVENTION

The fire department is another subdepartment
of the Chief Department of Security under the Executive Committee. As is true of the militia, it
too is covered in the local budget, but the fire
department has a subdivision for military fire security which is budgeted directly under the Union-
Republic Ministry of Security. Until 1963, the
Military Fire Security Subdivision was under the
Department for the Oktobrisky Railroad. The naval
base on the island of Kronshtadt has a separate
fire department.

The city fire department, in addition to fight-
ing fires, is responsible for training volunteer
fire brigades in each of the 350 housing committees
throughout the city and for inspection of compliance
with the city's fire regulations, which are set in
Moscow. The fire safety codes for buildings in
Leningrad are appallingly low by Western standards.
For example, there are no requirements for fire escapes or alternate stair wells, even for new, mul-
tistoried public buildings or apartment buildings,
and staircases in new apartment buildings have been
reduced in size by 25 to 30 per cent. Furthermore,
the age and construction of a large portion of the
buildings in the city's center make them fire traps.
The emphasis on total output has pushed the standard of fire safety to a very low level. Stress is
placed instead on preventive measures and training
of the population.

CULTURE AND EDUCATION

In matters of higher and advanced technical education, the city has no authority; the numerous training institutes and the University of Leningrad are operated under the Union-Republic Ministry of Higher and Special Middle Education. There are about 43 such schools, with an enrollment in 1963-64 of 232,400 students. In respect to primary education (the lower 8-year schools) and boarding schools, the city provides and maintains the physical plant and administration but has no authority over pedagogical affairs. The boarding schools, which as originally conceived by Khrushchev were to take over a large section of the educational system at the lower levels, now number only 61 in Leningrad, with an enrollment of 31,000 students and include a large number of specialized schools for disturbed, retarded children, children from broken homes, and other problem children.

The city's major responsibility in education lies in the operation of about 1,200 nursery schools and 500 crèches with an enrollment of 173,000 prenursery school children of working mothers. There are also 272 adult education schools (people's universities) under the city's jurisdiction with an enrollment of about 70,000 students. Most of these schools are administered through the various housing organizations which enlist help from the trade unions and Party.

In the area of culture the city operates 230 motion-picture theaters, 125 libraries, and a few theaters and museums. But most of the major museums, libraries, and theaters in Leningrad are operated directly by the R.S.F.S.R. Ministry of Culture or other central ministries. The 2,000 sports clubs, 11 cultural palaces, 18 stadiums, and 24 swimming pools are the responsibility of the city, working together with the Party and trade unions. Finally, the 11,070 hectares (27,342 acres) of parks and garden are city maintained and controlled. In the city proper, there are 4,070 hectares

(10,052 acres) of these parks, and 1,216 hectares (3,003 acres) of these are for general recreational purposes.

CONCLUSION

Chapters 2 and 3 discussed one method of escaping the formal structure of Leningrad's complex maze of local administration and control by the establishment of personal relations between city officials and officials in Moscow. Still another means is suggested by this overview of particular services: that is, to ignore or give only lip service to a large part of the overlapping responsibilities, coordinating devices, and inspection schemes, particularly the cumbersome arrangements involving the public. Though formally under a system of cross checks, various administrative units have developed considerable de facto independence in practice. This phenomenon is especially prevalent in departments where key personnel have had long tenure, are involved in straightforward operations, or are in less politically sensitive areas --such as departments of water and sewage, gas, bridges and roads, public transportation, or education. Even in such departments as housing, that deal with politically crucial questions and require more coordination, the tendency, in practice, has been to allow them the maximum possible autonomy. In discussing interdepartmental relations with individual city administrators, one is struck by the narrowness of their focus. They seem preoccupied only with the problems of their administrative bailiwick, and they avoid contact with other departments. Furthermore, department heads insist that they have a large amount of discretionary power at their disposal, in spite of numerous formal restrictions. Nevertheless, local administrators do not completely ignore the complex formal structure within which they must operate. They give it lip service, and more important, they discreetly manipulate various parts of the structure for their own purposes. Thus, for example, the militia makes

use of <u>druzhini</u> as much as possible to save money
and augment their meager forces, and the Executive
Committee uses the power of publicity against re-
calcitrant administrators under ministerial jurisdiction who refuse to do anything about air pollution. In conclusion, the coordination which the
structure and planning is supposed to provide is,
in fact, bypassed by personal relations or ignored
by compartmentalized administration.

NOTES TO CHAPTER 4

1. For housing and other related matters, the
U.S.S.R. is divided into four basic climatic zones:
Siberian, northwestern, central, and southern zones
with some special areas in Central Asia and along
the Black Sea. These zones are further divided into forty-seven subzones, of which fourteen are in
the R.S.F.S.R.

2. The procurator's office of Leningrad is
completely independent from the local government,
subordinate to the procurator of the republic.

3. Similar to the Water and Sewage Department
the Department of Gas Economy has had a stable administration, headed by Z. V. Solovoev since 1951.

4. <u>Leningradskaia gor. konferentsiia po okhra</u>
<u>atmosfernovo vozdukha</u> (<u>Leningrad City Conferenc</u>
<u>the Prevention of Atmospheric Pollution</u>) Lening
1963, p. 3.

5. <u>Ibid</u>., p. 28.

6. <u>Pravda</u>, October 3, 1966.

7. For production of live stock on individual
plots, see page 14.

8. See section in Chapter 3 on "Mass Participation in Local Government."

9. <u>Biulleten Ispolkmoa Lengorsoveta</u> [<u>Bulletin</u>
<u>of the Executive Committee of the Leningrad City</u>
<u>Soviet</u>], 1961, No. 15.

CHAPTER **5** HOUSING

THE ADMINISTRATIVE STRUCTURE

The largest and most extensive operation of the Leningrad city government is the construction and management of housing. A majority of the city's departments are directly or indirectly involved in the process. The Architect-Planning Department is the central office for the planning and development of new housing, in which it is aided by the city and rayon planning commissions. The actual construction of new housing is the task of the Chief Management of Housing, Civil and Industrial Construction, and to a lesser extent the Department of Capital Repairs. These departments in turn must be supplied by the Department of Construction Materials and are financially controlled by the State Construction Bank (Stroibank). Many of the other departments, such as Water and Sewage, Roads and Bridges, Gas, Tram and Trolley bus, Garden and Parks, Culture, Trade, General Provisions, Education, and Communications are brought in to provide necessary services to new housing areas. Such non-governmental bodies as the trade unions and the Party also have their assigned tasks in new housing construction. The Executive Committee and its coordinating committees on new construction are supposed to coordinate and plan the entire process. At the level of the R.S.F.S.R. and All Union governments are several organs that oversee the city Executive Committee's role and city agencies' performance, including Gosplan, the Committee for Construction, and the Ministries of Communal Economy, Construction, and Construction Materials.

Capital repairs to old housing structures are handled separately from new construction and entail greater local discretion. Even the funds come largely from locally controlled sources. The Executive Committee,together with the Departments of Housing, Capital Repairs, and Architect-Planning plan and approve capital repairs. They are under the general supervision, however, of the State Bank (Gosbank) and the R.S.F.S.R. Ministry of Communal Economy.

The management of housing once constructed is another separate operation and is primarily the concern of the Housing Management Department of the city and rayons aided by the Department of Cost and Distribution of Housing Space. Drawn into the task of management in various ways are also several of the city's service departments, the Committee on Physical Culture and Sports, and the Coordinating Committee on Youth Affairs, in addition to the trade unions.

BASIC HOUSING SUPPLY

In measuring housing space in the Soviet Union, account is traditionally taken of only the living area allocated to the individual. It ex- cludes kitchens, bathrooms, closets, and all corridors whether for general use or not. Such a measure was realistic when kitchens, bathrooms, and other facilities were largely shared. In most new housing, however, individual facilities are provided for each family and many Soviet writers feel that statistics should no longer be kept on the basis of housing or living space. They feel housing statistics should be measured in general usable space in each building. In this text, how- ever, figures are for housing space except where specifically indicated. Housing space represents approximately 65-70 per cent of general usable space.

Based on international standards, Soviet experts have recently set 9 square meters per person
as the minimum health requirement for housing space.
Since about 1930, the average housing space provided
in the cities of the Soviet Union, including Leningrad, has been about one half this minimum health
standard. In his long tenure of office, Stalin
made little or no effort to remedy this deficiency.

The revival of Leningrad as an important industrial center and the influx of population during
the First Five-Year Plan (1928-32) rapidly created
a housing shortage in the city. It was necessary
to reduce the minimum space per person from 4.5
spuare meters to 3.5 square meters. Although
Stalin was always reluctant to allocate resources
to consumer needs, it was necessary to construct
some new housing to accommodate the rapidly expanding population. Thus while in the 1920's, only
730,000 square meters of new housing had been constructed, in the 1930's about 2 million square
meters of housing space were built in Leningrad.
At the same time, the regime recognized the need to
stop further deterioration of the pre-Revolutionary
housing and increased expenditure on capital repairs fourfold. (See Table 20.) By 1941, the
total supply had reached 16.7 million square meters
of housing space, or about 5.4 square meters per
person. (See Table 19.) The Nazi siege of the
city reduced this to 13 million square meters by
1944. By 1946, 1.6 million square meters had been
restored; by 1956, an additional 791,000 square
meters had been rehabilitated, and 3.8 million
square meters of new housing had been built. This
brought the housing supply to a slightly higher
level than in 1941, but the average living space
per person remained low, about 5.5 square meters
per person. Furthermore, much of the housing was
substandard. Less than 25 per cent of the apartments had baths, and 16 per cent had only dark,
unventilated kitchens. Even in 1951, after the
new building program had begun in earnest, there
were only 235,900 apartments for 772,194 families--
an average of 3.3 families per apartment.

Beginning in 1956, the new Soviet leaders in
their appeal for mass support began to emphasize
nationwide construction of new housing and the
raising of basic dwelling standards. This had
strong appeal to the average citizen because lack
of decent housing had been his number-one complaint
since the war. Although no action by the regime
could have been more welcome, it was a long and
expensive process to relieve the shortage. Planners in Leningrad hoped to raise the average space
per person to 8.4 square meters by 1965, to 10.3
square meters by 1970, to 12.5 square meters by
1975, and to 15 square meters by 1880. The goal
proved to be overly ambitious, and by 1965 the
average space per person in Leningrad was only
about 7.2 square meters. Nevertheless, this was a
significant increase, and the seriousness of the
regime's intention is indicated by the accelerated
output of new housing since 1956. Tables 18
through 20 reflect this effort and additional
housing and construction statistics are given in
Tables 21-24.

Although the original plans called for continued high acceleration in housing output during
the 1960's, the pace proved more than the economic
system could bear. In 1962, there was an actual
drop in new housing, followed in subsequent years
by a more gradual increase in output. The decline
of population growth may also have influenced the
planners to reduce the pace of new construction in
Leningrad.

TABLE 18

New Housing Space in Leningrad and Suburbs, 1955-68

Year	Space Added (in 1,000 square meters)
1955	405
1956	441
1957	534
1958	735
1959	957
1960	1,100
1961	1,175
1962	1,170[*]
1963	1,360[*]
1964	1,260
1965	1,365
1966	1,530[**]
1967	1,380[**]
1968	1,516[**]

[*]Estimated.

[**]Planned.

Source: Compiled by author.

TABLE 19

Growth of Housing Stock in Leningrad Proper and Average Housing Space per Person

Year	Housing Space* (1,000 square meters)	General Usable Space* (1,000 square meters)	Square Meters per Person
1926	14,100	21,027	8.9
1928	14,421		
1932	15,601		
1937	16,182		
1940	16,450	25,700	5.4
1941	16,711		
1944	13,057		
1950	14,300	22,715	
1954		24,364	
1956		25,300	
1959	17,100	27,333	5.9
1960		28,852	
1961		30,544	
1962		32,372	
1963		34,064	
1964	22,800	36,571	7.1
1965	23,350	37,341	7.2

*See Page 112 for an explanation of housing space and general usable space.

Source: Compiled by author.

TABLE 20

Estimated Expenditures on Capital and Current Repairs of Housing in Leningrad

Years	Total Expenditure (Millions of rubles)	Average Expenditure per Year (Millions of rubles)
1929–32	9.1	2.3
1933–37	41.9	8.4
1938–40	39.6	13.2
1941–45*	--	--
1946–50	119.0	23.8
1951–55	188.0	37.6
1956	50.0	50.0
1962	54.0	54.0
1963	45.6	45.6
1964	48.9	48.9
1965	49.1**	49.1

*War years--figures not available.

**Projected.

Source: Compiled by author.

TABLE 21

Residential Buildings in Leningrad Proper, 1956

No. of Stories in Residential Buildings	Per Cent of Total	Age of Buildings	Per Cent of Total
1	.8	0-50	41.0
2	4.3	50-100	27.8
3	9.2	100-150	7.3
4	24.4	More than 150	1.8
5 or more	61.3	Unknown	22.2

Source: Gorodskoe khoziaistvo [The City's Economy] (Leningrad, 1957), p. 30.

118

TABLE 22

Average Costs for Construction of New Housing Space:
Two Studies in the Moscow Area, 1965

(Cost in rubles per square meter of housing space)

No. of Stories	Construction Costs	Costs of Developing All Services and Garden Parks	Total Costs	Basic Norm of Housing Space per Hectare of Land (Square meters)
5	117	47.0	164.0	3,100
9	125	36.2	161.7	4,100
12	142	32.6	174.6	4,600

Source: Ekonomika stroitelstva (The Economics of Construction), No. 4 (1965), p. 55.

(Cost in rubles per square meter of housing space)

No. of Stories	Construction Costs	Basic Engineering Costs	Cultural and Daily Services	Connecting Utilities	Total
4	121.7	44.0	16.3	52.8	234.8
5	117.6	38.9	15.5	46.8	219.8
9	122.4	29.7	14.7	36.0	202.8

Source: Arkhitektura S.S.S.R. (Architecture U.S.S.R.), No. 1 (1965), p. 22.

TABLE 23

Average Monthly Pay of Housing Construction Workers
in the Soviet Union, 1961

Category of Worker	Rubles
Painter	88
Mason	96
Plasterer	96
Stone worker	97
Carpenter	100
Electrician	105
Metal worker	105
Steel Worker	108
Concrete assembler	133

Source: Voprosi proizvoditelnosti truda
[Questions of Labor Productivity] (Leningrad, 1962),
p. 32.

TABLE 24

Housing Offices Operating in Leningrad, 1956

No. of Offices	Amount of Housing Space Controlled by Each Office (in 1,000's of square meters)	Operating Losses Sustained (Average rubles per square meter)
110	Up to 5	16.5
271	5-10	8.6
683	10-15	3.0
98	15-20	3.0
10	20-25	2.4
6	25 or more	--

Source: D. L. Broner, Sovremennie problem zhilishchnovo khoziaistva [Contemporary Problems of the Housing Economy] (Moscow, 1961), p. 190.

PLANNING

When the general economy was decentralized into economic regions in 1957, the planning and construction of new housing was also decentralized.
A new Department of Housing, Civil and Industrial
Construction was created under the Executive Committee in Leningrad. It was soon discovered,
however, that decentralization created a chaotic
situation in respect to building supplies and a
serious inequality in the distribution of construction capital (already in short supply) caused by
the superior affluence of some regions. Thus, in
1959, all planning of construction was recentralized under the State Committee on Construction
Affairs of the U.S.S.R. Council of Ministers. For
the purpose of administration, construction allocations are currently administered through the
republics and their ministries. In the case of the
R.S.F.S.R., the republic is subdivided into climatic zones for planning and into regions for construction. Leningrad is the experimentation head-
quarters for the northwestern climatic area. Most
of the test projects are planned and carried out
by the research institute, LenZNIIEP, which works
closely with the city's Architect-Planning Department, the Architect-Technical Soviet of Leningrad,
and the Union of Architects of both Leningrad and
Moscow. The Architect-Technical Soviet of Leningrad is a council of the city's leading architects
and construction engineers; they advise on new
projects, experiments, and techniques. LenZNIIEP
is directly responsible to the U.S.S.R. State Construction Committee. There is also another experimental institute, LenNIIP, which tests construction materials.

In spite of the recentralization in 1959,
construction planning in the Leningrad area was
divided and confused until 1961. The city planned
between 30-35 per cent of all building. The
Leningrad Sovnarkhoz (the economic region encompassing the city of Leningrad and the Leningrad

Oblast during 1957-65)planned 23 per cent, and the various ministries operating in the area planned 40-45 per cent. Then, after 1961, all capital outlays from the state budget for housing, communal services, culture, welfare, and trade were distributed through the city. The sovnarkhoz and ministries continued to carry out housing and communal services financed from their planned and unplanned profits allocated to housing and workers' welfare. In 1965, only 350,000 square meters of housing were planned from capital resources not allocated through the city, and the completed construction with such resources was less. By 1965, the abolition of the sovnarkhozes further simplified planning; then, in 1966, all housing construction in Leningrad came under the city's management with very few exceptions.

Except for experimentation, the key responsibility for the planning of housing and communal buildings falls on the Architect-Planning Department. The department is attached to the Executive Committee but is responsible to the State Committee on Construction (Gostroi) of the U.S.S.R. Council of Ministers. It is a large department and employs several thousand people. In addition to the usual administrative sections, it is divided into several basic divisions, such as: an office for the general plan; a section for the repair of historic buildings (whose work is discussed in detail in a later section); an office for construction of general public buildings; the technical inspector's office to check on the fulfillment of plans and safety regulations; the state architect bureau, which draws up building specifications; and the subordinate institute, Lenproekt, which draws up the working plans. Lenproekt itself employs over 1,000 people and is divided into sections covering such matters as sanitation, gas, sewage, and historic buildings. Each section has its own inspectors to check fulfillment. The Architect-Planning Department also has offices headed by a chief architect in each of the rayons.

As the first step in planning, interested
parties such as <u>rayons</u> and housing cooperatives
must submit a yearly request for buildings by
September 1, to the Architect-Planning Department.
Regardless of their organizational status, enterprises in Leningrad that feel they need additional
housing for their workers must apply to the Department of Architect-Planning. Unlike other cities
in the Soviet Union, new housing requested by various enterprises is not turned over to them after
completion for operation and control, but is
managed by the city of Leningrad. The Architect-
Planning Department takes the requests together
with its own building plans and draws up a tentative plan for the city in the form of a "title
list." Although the preliminary planning is
centered in the Architect-Planning Department,
many other organizations are consulted. Most important is the Presidium of the Executive Committee, which apparently works very closely with the
Architect-Planning Department. Furthermore, there
is a coordinating construction subcommittee of
the Executive Committee, composed of the Executive
Committee chairman (who also serves as the subcommittee chairman), and eleven members from the
various departments connected with construction.

As mentioned earlier, no building can be
constructed in Leningrad without approval from the
head of the Architect-Planning Department. His
control over industrial building, however, is
restricted to designating where it can be built
and some of the exterior features. In housing,
however, his control is more extensive and it is
backed by the Executive Committee which also must
pass on all new housing in the city, even that
being built by organizations not under its control.
In the latter case, if the Executive Committee
disagrees, it must give its reasons and disagree-
ment is arbitrated in Moscow.

On major projects affecting the whole city,
the Architect-Technical Soviet of Leningrad must
be consulted. But for less important projects,

even if they are not under the city's jurisdiction,
the Expert-Technical Section of the Architect-
Planning Department must pass on the building. The
Expert-Technical Section must in turn consult and
clear projects with the Departments of Fire, Sanitation, Trade, Parks and Gardens, Public and Communal Services, Welfare, and Enlightenment.

Other voices at the preliminary planning stage
come from the State Construction Bank (Stroibank),
which must pass on the financial aspects of the
plan, and the Department of Housing, Civil and
Industrial Construction. These organizations have
an influence on the type, cost, and scheduling of
building. Significantly, the departments that are
not consulted in the planning stage are the departments which manage the housing or buildings once
they are completed.

Depending on the cost of a building, various
levels of government have discretion to change and
approve projects in the preliminary plans. Of new
projects, the city's Executive Committee can approve projects of less than 200,000 rubles; for
projects of 200,000 to 500,000 rubles, the Executive Committee's approval must be verified by
Gosplan of the R.S.F.S.R. For projects of 500,000
to 1 million rubles, the approval of the R.S.F.S.R.
Gosplan is required. Between 1 million and 2.5
million rubles the R.S.F.S.R. Gosplan decides but
with the verification of the U.S.S.R. Gosplan.
Above 2.5 million rubles, the decision of the
U.S.S.R. Gosplan is necessary.

For changes in plans or location of buildings,
the city's Executive Committee can make decisions
on projects up to 1 million rubles, but Moscow
must approve other changes.

The final negotiations for the two-year plan
and yearly plan of construction are conducted by the
Architect-Planning Department, the Department of Housing, Civil and Industrial Construction, the Presidium,
and other city elite, with Gosplan, the Ministries of

Construction and the U.S.S.R. Committee on Construction (Gostroi) in Moscow. Once these negotiations
have been completed, a final "title list" for all
new buildings is drawn up and passed by the City's
Executive Committee and approved by the R.S.F.S.R.
Council of Ministers. Then, on the basis of this
list,Lenproekt draws up the working plans and a pass
port (building permit) is issued for each building.

Although Leningrad is more fortunate than
other cities in being able to build and control
its own housing, like other cities except for
Moscow, it has little leeway in being able to ex-
periment or construct special housing projects.
The literature is full of numerous special and new
types of buildings proposed by the various Leningrad engineering and architectural institutes, but
few are actually built, compared to Moscow, where
institutes in recent years have constructed a
number of monumental buildings and experimental
projects. This situation is surprising, as Leningrad is the second most important cultural center
in the U.S.S.R., contains one of the oldest and
most famous training schools for architects and
engineers (the Leningrad Engineering Construction
Institute founded in 1830), and has a large number
of architects. Nevertheless, the overwhelming
strength in the field of architecture is in Moscow.
Out of a total of 10,462 members of the Union of
Architects, Moscow has 3,640 architects compared to
1,248 in Leningrad, and the Union of Architects
is dominated by the Moscow members. For example,
in 1965, its Executive Committee had 129 architects:
57 from Moscow, 9 from Leningrad, and 10 from the
Ukraine. Its presidium and top policy-making body
had 26 members, of which there were 12 from Moscow,
1 from Leningrad, and 1 from each of the union
republics.[1]

There is also a basic economic reason for not
allowing individual building design in Leningrad.
Mass building costs average about 123 rubles per
square meter of housing space, while the cheapest
individually constructed apartment building costs
average 166 rubles per square meter, and others go

as high as 300 rubles. As a result, while the
Soviet leadership in the last decade has been
sprucing up Moscow with several new monumental
buildings and making it a show capital, Leningrad
has been designated as a provincial city of only
historical and industrial interest. Construction
has been routine, including prefabricated housing
and a minimum number of general public buildings,
except for the restoration of pre-Revolutionary
historical monuments in the area. For example, in
1964, the Leningrad press based a great deal of
propaganda on the opening of a new, modern, multi-
storied hotel, the Rossiia, on the avenue to the
airport; in fact, it is a very routine structure,
suffering from poor quality and antiquated equipment.

As mentioned earlier, the basic planning areas
for housing in Leningrad are the living rayon,
microrayon, and housing block. The primary unit is
the housing block of between 2,000 and 3,000
people. The apartments in the housing block are
located within a radius of about 200 meters from a
central area, which is planned to contain a garden,
a play area, one or more community rooms, a nursery
school, a creche, and one or more food stores. The
next higher unit is the microrayon. In Leningrad,
they vary in size from 30 to 70 hectares (74 to
173 acres) with a radius of about 400 to 700
meters. In the older, crowded parts of the city,
or where apartment houses are over five stories,
the microrayons often replace the housing block as
the primary unit or organization. In addition to
the facilities of the housing block, the microrayon contains a cafeteria, some repair services,
a general produce store, club rooms for youth and
the aged, and a housing office.

The living rayon is composed of several microrayons and has a population of 25,000 to 30,000,
within a radius of about two thirds of a mile.
Planned in the central area of the living rayon
are a green area for a small stadium, sports
fields, an open air theater, a library, and administrative offices. Trade facilities in the

living rayon include a department store, specialty
stores, and branch offices for communal and public
services. This pattern of living areas has been
imposed where possible on both the old and new
areas of Leningrad. Judging from complaints, the
main deficiency has been the failure to provide
the proper retail and telephone services in each
unit. It was reported in a new section of Leningrad, with 100,000 people, that there was no
theater of any kind, no house of culture, no
sports club, and no restaurants, cafeterias, hospitals, department stores, or adequate transport.[2]

Until recently, no attention was given in
Soviet planning to the value of land; as a result,
Soviet city planners in new areas provided large
park areas around new apartment buildings. The
State Committee on Architecture in Moscow subsequently prescribed minimum limits on the amount of
space around new developments. Even though no
monetary value is assigned to the land in figuring
construction costs and no land rent is included in
calculating operational costs, the expense of
maintaining garden areas (figured at a minimum of
10 kopeks per square meter) and the extra cost of
extending services tend to hold planners to the
minimum garden space required. By Western standards this is still considerable. If land is assigned a value, as some Soviet economists advocate,
and as the land close to the cities becomes crowded,
the large park areas may in time be reduced. But
the broad avenues and ample gardens give the new
areas a spacious, pleasant look. The main difficulty is that the gardens are usually poorly kept.
Funds for professional maintenance are minimal;
their upkeep depends on the voluntary work of the
local inhabitants and is not forthcoming without
extensive organization and pressure.

A more serious problem with the new areas
mushrooming around the city is the inadequacy of
design for new housing. It is possible to argue,
using Western standards for modern housing, that
the Soviet regime is only building new slums. The

continued shortage of metal and lack of funds, for
example, have caused designers to use wood of the
poorest quality for windows and doors, which do
not fit and warp almost immediately. Furthermore,
in cutting costs they have designed panels so thin
that there is a high transfer of noise and heat.
Jokes and songs about noise and temperatures in
new apartment buildings are plentiful. All of the
rooms, from the living room to the bath, are small.
Although in the present housing shortage small-
roomed apartments fulfill an important need, when
the city moves to a standard of 15 square meters
per person these apartments will be considered
inadequate and uncomfortable. Finally, the stress
on low cost has created completely utilitarian and
monotonous buildings, and an unpleasant sameness
pervades the entire Soviet Union.

CONSTRUCTION

The reform of 1962 took construction entirely
out of the hands of the sovnarkhozes and created
regional construction organizations. In the
western part of the R.S.F.S.R., this regional organization is Zapadstroi. But Leningrad itself is
such an important construction area that it has its
own department for construction, Chief Management
for Housing, Civil and Industrial Construction
(Glavleningradstroi), directly responsible to the
R.S.F.S.R. Ministry of Construction and attached
to the city's Executive Committee. In 1962, it
had a labor force of 48,200 and has continued to
expand since then. The actual work of construction
is divided among various combinats and trusts under
the department.

Before 1959, all construction was carried out
by trusts, each dealing with a separate phase of
the building process such as the foundation, basic
structure, plumbing, and finishing. Then, in
1959, Leningrad created the first housing combinat
in the Soviet Union. Combinats are so structured
that each one can perform all the processes for

construction, from the basic building materials
to the completed building.   This method of operation is particularly suitable for prefabricated
buildings and has become standard practice in the
Soviet Union.   (See Chart 7.)   Six combinats in
Leningrad do the major portion of the building.
They accounted for 65 per cent of the communal
building in 1962.   Five of the combinats primarily
build apartment houses; the sixth builds schools,
theaters, and so forth.   The trusts under the
Department of Capital Repairs attached to the
Executive Committee also build new housing, most of
which are individual projects.   For example, in
1962 they constructed 46.8 million rubles of new
housing or between 12-13 per cent of the total.

Beginning in the 1940's, but becoming particularly important after the death of Stalin, Soviet
builders began experimenting with and using prefabricated methods of construction.   The system
has rapidly become the dominant method of construction for new urban housing.   In Leningrad,
prefabs accounted for 5 per cent of housing construction in 1955, 54 per cent in 1960, and 69
per cent in 1961.

The first type of prefabricated building
widely used was the large block building.   It is
composed of cast or mortared masonry blocks
embedded with steel hooks for lifting.   Large
cranes running on tracks parallel to the building
hoist the blocks into place.   The fit of these
blocks is rather crude, and frequently the blocks
are badly chipped or cracked by the time they have
been fixed into place.   These cracks and chips are
then cemented over, but the sealing and patching
inevitably begin to fall out within a year, due to
changes in temperature.

CHART 7

Housing Construction Apparatus in Leningrad

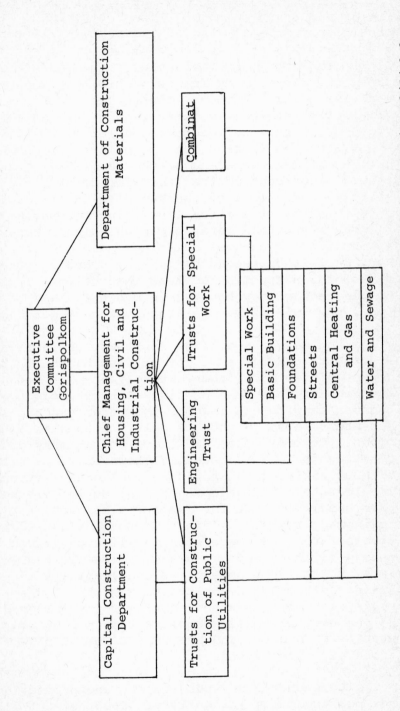

Based on: Balmakova, I. K. et. al. Finansirovanie i rascheti v zhilishchnom stroitelstve (Financing and Cost of Housing Construction), Leningrad and Moscow: 1961, p. 7.

131

As construction became better organized, a
faster and easier method of prefabricating became
possible; this new method relied principally on
large panels of reinforced concrete. Each wall or
floor of a room forms one panel. As needed, the
panels include window frames, doors, and internal
conduits. For bathrooms, the entire room is prefabricated into one unit, including all facilities.
The panels are manufactured at a large assembly
plant and then trucked out to the site of the new
building. Manufacturing of the panels accounts for
about 40 per cent of the labor for constructing the
building. The cost of these prefab buildings is
much less than traditional building methods and
slightly less than large block building. More
important, large panel buildings have cut the
amount of labor needed by one third and cut the
time for construction to less than half.[3] In 1965,
65 per cent of new housing in Leningrad was of this
type. By 1968 it was to account for 86 per cent.

Each year the designs for these prefabricated
apartments undergo some change, but basically they
do not differ much from year to year. In height
the emphasis has been on five-story buildings
because they do not require the added expense of
elevators (also in short supply) or special founda-
tions. Cutting costs is always the primary goal in
construction. More recently, however, as a result
of cost analyses on providing public and communal
services to new developments, the Soviet planners
have concluded that for large cities such as
Leningrad, taller buildings up to nine and twelve
stories are as or more economical, even though the
actual building cost is higher. (See Table 22.)
Thus, since 1965, several of the combinats in
Leningrad have been constructing highrise apartments of nine to sixteen stories. In Leningrad,
33 per cent of housing constructed in 1965 was nine
stories or higher, and by 1968, 73 per cent was
expected to be highrise.

The emphasis on speed, cost, and production
has meant sacrificing quality. The theme of all

the periodical literature on housing in Leningrad
and elsewhere has been the need to improve quality.
For example, one periodical reported that as high
as 60 per cent of housing construction was defec-
tive.[4] There seems to be several reasons for the
poor quality of construction. One factor is the
high turnover of labor in the construction industry,
an annual average of 30 per cent in Leningrad. The
pattern of employment for young engineers and ap-
prentices is to work in home construction to gain
some experience and then move on to higher-paying
jobs in heavy industry as they become available.
(See Table 23.)

According to Soviet writers, the planning
process also has serious deficiencies. Cost estimates are often 10-15 per cent off. In a study of
Leningrad's housing construction plans made in
1961, the investigators found 152 mistakes totaling
10 million rubles. In the same year, the housing
plan was changed 40 times in major categories and
750 times in minor categories. Also in the case
of the 1961 plan, 32.3 per cent of buildings were
not completed by the end of the year, although the
maximum allowable proportion of noncompletion was
only 20.6 per cent.

Other reasons for the lack of quality in
housing are the absence of good indices and the
failure of numerous inspectors to demand high
standards. For example, the State Construction
Bank (Stroibank) not only is active in the planning stage of housing but also controls the expenditures during construction. It approves payment at various intervals after inspections, but
its main concern is that the work be done and not
that the quality of the product be high. The same
is true with the other inspectors from the Party,
the peoples' state commissions, the trade unions,
and the city. Although special inspection commissions have been set up by trade unions to oversee quality, these commissions seem powerless
and/or unwilling to resist the primary standard of
success in the Soviet Union--fulfillment of

production goals and winning the numbers game.
Trade unions are probably the weakest organizations to rely on for this task, because in general
they have not been effective overseers of government operations. The city, which is the recipient
of the buildings, has also been a poor watchdog
because its inspectors come on the scene when it is
really too late.[5] Articles have suggested that
city inspectors become involved earlier, but the
lack of manpower and the city's inability to alter
methods without tremendous effort do not hold out
much hope for this solution.

In the latter part of the 1950's and early
1960's, the emphasis was on mechanization which
hopefully would reduce the need for labor, reduce
the costs, and raise the quality. In fact, a
special technical department under the city's
Executive Committee was established in 1964 to
deal with this problem. It accomplished the first
two tasks quite well, but in respect to quality of
construction it has done little except for some
improvement of the basic prefab units. The planners have found it difficult to mechanize the
finishing work that is essential to high quality.
The stress on mechanization as the solution is
still strongly emphasized, but it is doubtful how
much more can be mechanized, and mechanization
cannot solve the basic problems of quality.

More recently, the major effort to raise
standards has been a search for adequate quality
indices which are both high enough and measurable,
and which the regime might be willing to adopt as
a basic criteria of success. However, this has
only been discussed in the literature, and nothing
useful as yet seems to have been proposed. The
one area where quality control seems to operate
in construction has been in cooperative housing.

COOPERATIVE HOUSING

Private housing has never played an important
role in Soviet cities. In suburban and rural

areas, however, it has been possible to construct
individual homes with some government help. Leningrad has made small housing plots available in
restricted areas on the outer fringes of the city
for which a homeowner pays only a modest land rent.
In addition, it was possible to borrow up to 60 per
cent of the cost of construction from government
banks, for a ten-year period, at 1 per cent interest. The major reason that private housing construction was never extensive was not the lack of
funds but the inability to find workmen and materials. For the most part, a potential houseowner
had to either build it himself or hire workers
after hours. But even more difficult was the
problem of finding building materials which have
been in perpetual short supply. The regime itself
did little or nothing to make materials available
to individuals. The regime's argument against
more support for individual housing has been the
high cost of construction and of supplying
services to individual homes, and the rapid
depreciation of private wooden dwellings compared
to concrete and brick multiple dwellings. More
recently, in cities like Leningrad, authorities
have also argued that single-home construction
entailed waste of valuable space. Within Leningrad proper, private homes have never accounted
for more than 1 per cent of the housing space,
but in the suburban area, private dwellings are
more plentiful, about 25 per cent. Many of these
are the summer cottages of the more well-to-do in
the city. In 1956, individual dwellings accounted
for 2.8 per cent of housing space for the city as
a whole.

Another form of private dwelling which the
regime has encouraged from time to time is the
housing cooperative (ZhSK). Housing cooperatives
were actively encouraged and partially government-
financed in the 1920's, but this development was
brought to an abrupt end with their confiscation
and placement under government operation in 1937.
After World War II, the idea was halfheartedly
reactivated, and the cooperatives suffered the
same inability to secure building materials as

private owners. They had the additional disadvan-
tage of not having government loans available to
them. After Stalin's death, they were more actively encouraged, but it still took from three to
five years to complete their buildings. As a result,
by 1962, only twelve housing cooperatives had been
formed in Leningrad. But of the two forms of
private dwellings, the latter has come to be increasingly preferred by post-Stalin regimes. This
preference is closely related to the growing
shortage of investment capital and the accumulation
of consumer spending power. Cooperatives are a
means of putting these excess consumer resources to
good use.

A major drive to organize new housing cooperatives was launched in 1962. Other socialist governments in Eastern Europe had already led the way by
initiating major programs of cooperative housing
several years previously. In 1962, for the first
time, Soviet planners included cooperatives in the
basic materials plan and gave them an equal priority with other housing projects in the capital construction plan. The trade unions and the city
were ordered to take an active lead in organizing
the new cooperatives; this had formerly been a
responsibility of the Leningrad Department of Construction. At the same time, one-family dwellings
in cities were prohibited, and even in suburban
areas it became increasingly difficult to get
permission to build private homes. In this way,
the planners hoped to direct private funds into
cooperative housing. In Leningrad, citizens who
have lived in the city for 10 years and have a
full-time position can become members of a cooperative. Each cooperative is made up of 60 members
and is formed into a legal corporate unit run, in
theory, by the membership. The members must pay
down 40 per cent of the cost of construction, and
the government lends them the remainder for 10-15
years at 1 per cent interest. (Overdue accounts
are charged 3 per cent interest.) The average
total cost of a one-room apartment of from 12 to
20 square meters is 2,800-4,100 rubles. The

maximum size anyone can purchase is 60 square
meters, regardless of the size of his family. With
this new encouragement, 156,000 square meters of
cooperative housing were constructed in Leningrad
in 1963; 330,000 square meters in 1964; and 387,000
square meters in 1965.

Although Leningrad has not quite fulfilled
its plan in respect to cooperative housing, it has
had a much better record (95-97 per cent) than most
Soviet cities. On the one hand, the large down-
payment, the red tape in organization, and the
delay in supplying such services as telephones
(requiring almost a two-year wait), has made the
organization of new cooperatives difficult. On the
other hand, there are several features of cooperative apartments that make them attractive to the
population. Most important, a family does not have
to wait indefinitely for a new apartment. In
Leningrad, a family or individual cannot even apply
for a new apartment from the city unless his current accommodations are less than 4.5 square meters
per person. In addition, for a couple or a single
person, the cooperative apartment is almost the
only way to avoid sharing a room or apartment. For
every one-room apartment in Leningrad today, there
are at least four couples or individuals who would
like such an apartment. Finally, the quality of
cooperative housing is better than public housing,
even though the designs are the same. From the
very beginning, the individual owners check on the
construction of their buildings, and by a combina-
tion of cajoling and extra payments, they are able
to raise the quality of workmanship.

In conclusion, cooperative apartments have
come to play an important role in housing construction and will probably continue to do so. It is
true, of course, that cooperative apartments may
again be confiscated as they were in 1937, and
many owners of the new cooperatives are aware of
this, but they are not very concerned, because what
they are purchasing in their own minds is not a
private piece of property but the right to live in

a decent apartment. This right of occupancy has
been traditionally respected in the Soviet Union
and is protected by a whole body of law and prece-
dent. It is one of the few areas where the legal
system in Soviet society is meaningful and rigidly
practiced. Furthermore, the rents in public
housing and the maintenance costs for cooperatives
are about the same. Thus, once an individual has
the right to occupy a certain apartment, he does
not care too much who actually owns the building.

RESTORATION OF HISTORIC MONUMENTS

     Although Leningrad has been denied much in
the way of funds for building new public monuments
and experimenting in new housing projects, large
sums, even under Stalin, were allocated for the
restoration of pre-Revolutionary monuments damaged
in World War II. As Leningraders themselves admit,
the leaders wanted to turn the city's center into
a large museum, and today, the tourist walking
along the Neva and in the older sections of the
city, can almost believe he is in imperial Russia
of the nineteenth century. It is estimated that
Leningrad has 750 architectural monuments and 150
historic buildings; 800 of these are in the center
of the city.

     The amount spent on restoration of public
buildings and palaces around Leningrad has been
200 million rubles since World War II and the work
is still not completed. For example, the whole
interior of Petrodvorets (Peter's Versailles-like
palace in the suburbs), is yet to be restored.
Immediately after the war, special sections of the
Architect-Planning Department and the Lenproekt
Institute were created to handle restoration. One
major difficulty was that in 1945 there were only
30 craftsmen who were capable of carrying out the
restoration, and it became necessary to train a
whole new workforce. Today, there are 600 skilled
craftsmen, but even so the work is slow and costly.
The restoration work is overseen by the State
Inspector for the Preservation of Historic Places
in Moscow.

CAPITAL REPAIRS

Capital repairs of older housing in a city
like Leningrad, where 40 per cent of the housing
stock is over 50 years old, is as important as new
construction. (See Table 21.) In the center of the
city, the government wants to maintain the old fa-
cade but at the same time make the buildings usable.
But even in less historic areas the shortage has been
so great that old buildings are rarely torn down. The
Soviet leadership's policy has always been to
modernize old buildings as funds become available,
with little regard for cost. In 1959, on an
average, capital repairs in the Soviet Union cost
85 rubles per square meter while new housing cost
105-10 rubles per square meter. Some repair costs
reached as high as 117-50 rubles per square meter.
In Moscow, capital repairs were even more expensive
than new housing: 122 rubles per square meter
compared to only 117 rubles per square meter for
new construction. Within the last few years, for
the first time, writers have begun to question the
value of reconstruction when the cost is equal to
and in some cases greater than new housing.

In Leningrad, the task of capital repairs is
performed by the Department of Capital Repairs for
Housing of the Executive Committee. In this area
of construction, the city is more autonomous than
in new construction and does not merely receive
the end product. Although the budget and standards
for capital repairs are set in Moscow, the actual
allocation and supervision is done by the city.
Theoretically, the cost of capital repairs is included in the rent of the building. In fact, the
actual cost of maintenance plus current and capital
repairs for housing is universally greater than the
rent collected. Only in the case of rent collected
by the city from enterprises occupying its buildings does the rent more closely approximate costs.
Thus, the amount contributed from rent to the
capital-repair fund is small and has to be heavily
subsidized each year. In Leningrad, subsidization

out of the city budget for 1956 amounted to 90 per cent of the expenditure for capital repairs. Most enterprises operating their own housing must subsidize capital repairs by 100 per cent.

The Department of Capital Repairs for Housing is divided into various trusts and enterprises. Before World War II, twenty-eight repair trusts were attached to the housing bureaus in each rayon. After the war, they were organized into seventeen bureaus spread throughout the city and suburbs. In 1950, a single Department of Capital Repairs was created and the various repair and technical trusts were put under its over-all control. There are now eighteen general repair-construction trusts that work directly under the offices of repair-construction in each rayon housing department. For the city as a whole, there are repair trusts for facades, elevators and nonliving space, and special enterprises or sections for transport, mechanization, plastering, sanitation, hardware, and so forth. Also associated with the department is the experimental institute for capital repairs, LNIIAKh, which is a Leningrad affiliate of the Academy of Communal Economy in Moscow.

Even before the regime decided to expand the output of new housing in the 1950's, it increased expenditures on repairs and modernization as the first step to improve housing conditions. Thus by 1955 expenditure by the Leningrad capital repair trusts had expanded 2.1 times. Today, the outlay for capital repairs is over 50 million rubles per year but represents only about 25-30 per cent of the expenditure for new housing. Current annual plans for capital repairs in Leningrad designate 200,000-210,000 square meters of housing space for renewal. Except for one year between 1960 and 1965, however, the plan was not fulfilled.

When an apartment is ready for capital repairs, the wear and tear has already brought about a 50-60 per cent depreciation of its value or usefulness. A 1960 study of the buildings about

to be repaired produced the following statistics:
The average living space per person in the buildings was 6.78 square meters, and there were 3.45
families per apartment; only 21.5 per cent of the
apartments had bathrooms, and only 20 per cent of
the buildings had central heating. Thus, by
Western standards, the time for capital repairs
and improvements for much of Soviet housing is
long overdue.

     As in the case of new construction, the major
problem with capital repairs is quality, and it is
a constant theme in the literature. A study made
in 1958-59 of a series of newly renovated apartments revealed that 76 per cent of the renovation
was below standard and, as discussed previously,
Russian standards are not high. An extreme example
of the poor quality was the complete collapse in
May, 1966, of a newly renovated apartment building
in the central part of Leningrad. The causes for
low quality are much the same as those in new
construction, including frequent turnover of personnel. For example, in 1965, out of 13,504
workers, 3,541 left and 3,932 were hired. The
favorite remedy in recent years, as in new construction, has been a stress on mechanization, but
repairs are not easily mechanized and the effort
has had little effect on quality. Efforts have
also been made to give guarantees for the work
but, except in extreme cases, these seem to have
little effect.

     General redecorating and repairs within an
apartment are the tenant's responsibility. He can
hire a repair trust or find individuals, but he
must pay the costs himself, although the banks
will lend him money for this purpose. The tenant
may borrow for repairs if the cost is over 30
rubles and after he has paid down 20 per cent. If
the cost is equal to two months of his salary, he
has six months to pay; if it is equal to four
months of his salary, he is given twelve months to
pay.

RENTS

The Soviet system has always prided itself on
the low rents that the population is charged. On
an average, rent is not more than 4-5 per cent of
a family's income; an extra charge is made for
utilities. The rent schedule is more or less
uniform throughout the U.S.S.R. and was established
in 1924 with some modifications up to 1937.[6]
Since 1937, the rent scale has remained constant
except for nonresidential space, that is, space
rented to retail shops, services, enterprises, and
various organizations. The city soviet, through
the housing bureaus, signs a lease for up to five
years with each tenant. This is a mere formality,
however, and at the end of the lease period it is
automatically renewed. A tenant can only be removed from his housing space by court action and
then only for a serious violation of the lease or
a housing regulation.

The amount of rent collected from individual
tenants does not cover costs. Often it does not
even pay for maintenance and current repairs. The
average rent per square meter of housing space in
the Soviet Union for the years 1959-62 was 1.47
rubles per year. The average current expenditures
were 1.88 rubles per square meter, and the costs
of capital repairs were 4.90 rubles per square
meter. In Leningrad in 1962, the average rent was
1.58 rubles, current expenditures were 1.72 rubles,
and capital repairs were 2.30 rubles. In contrast
to the rent from housing, the rent schedule for
nonresidential space is based on actual costs,
although it is argued by some Soviet writers that
the depreciation rates used are unrealistically
low. In the same way, the charges for gas,
electricity, water, and heat both for living and
nonliving space are based on actual cost and
usually allow utilities to be self-sufficient.
(Most of the rates for utilities are set locally
and merely approved by Moscow.)

The unrealistic rents for housing create some
serious problems. Paying such low rents, tenants
are discouraged from complaining about poor conditions because the perennial answer is that there
is not enough money. Furthermore, the city government, which has a low priority status in the system and is always short of funds, has a difficult
time subsidizing housing and is pressured to reduce maintenance costs to the barest minimum, often
just to the point of keeping the elements from
completely destroying the building. In addition,
the city's burden is increasing as the amount of
housing increases. Even in new buildings, where
the cost of maintenance is lower, the rents collected are not sufficient to cover costs and have
to be subsidized. Thus, except for the propaganda
value of having low rents, there seems to be no
practical economic value for the unrealistic rates,
because the population must indirectly pay anyway.
Certainly Westerners examining Soviet housing are
not impressed by the low rents. The increased
discussions in periodicals of the large gap between income and costs in housing, the recent
revision of rent schedules for nonresidential
space, the growing interest in drawing off some of
the excess buying power of the population, and the
gradual moves to equate cost and prices in the
over-all economic system may in time bring a revision in rents. It could be argued that an increase of 50 per cent would still put rents well
below those in capitalist countries and would con-
stitute about the same percentage of a worker's
salary spent on rent as in 1940. For example, in
1940, a Leningrad family spent 5.4 per cent of its
income on rent and in 1956, 3.8 per cent. When he
was still in power, Khrushchev alluded to the need
and his intention to raise rents. It is likely
that his successors, who have generally followed
his program, but at a slower pace, will in time
raise the rent schedules.

MAINTENANCE ORGANIZATION

Control and management of housing in the
U.S.S.R. is of three types. First, there are individual homes, mostly in small towns and villages,
which are maintained by individuals organized into
street committees for control and over-all maintenance under the local soviet. The second group is
housing controlled and operated by the local government through district housing bureaus. This category includes city-owned housing and the newly-
formed cooperatives. In almost all cases, the
cooperatives in the large cities are organized by
local government and trade union authorities, and
they contract for their maintenance with the local
government. The third group is housing built and
controlled by various industries, institutes, and
departments not attached to local government.
Industry-owned housing has always been important in
recruiting and attracting skilled labor, because a
better apartment is cherished more highly than a
raise in pay. Housing controlled by industries,
institutes, and centralized departments account for
the bulk of urban housing: 68 per cent in 1962,
throughout the Soviet Union. The 1957 administrative reforms had set one goal as the control of all
housing by local government. It was stressed that
housing management detracted from the main purpose
of industry and that experience had proved that
local governments on an average could operate
housing more cheaply. But industries and central
departments were not persuaded that this was good
economic rationalization and clung to their control
of housing. In any struggle for power, the centralized bureau or industry is bound to win. As a
result, these organizations not only have continued
to control their own housing but have built a large
portion of new housing.

The Leningrad city government has been fortunate in having inherited all the pre-Revolutionary
housing that, until recently, constituted the bulk
of housing in Leningrad. As a result, in 1956,

73.3 per cent of the housing was operated by the city, compared to only 57 per cent in Moscow. Also, with respect to new construction, the city has continued to maintain its control and received about three quarters of all new housing built.

Although the reform of 1957 never brought about any actual change in the administration of housing in the U.S.S.R., articles arguing for control of housing by local government did not cease and apparently were encouraged by the regime. As a result, the post-Khrushchev leadership, in its usual cautious manner, is beginning to push the reform forward. Leningrad is the first recipient of this slow change. On August 23, 1965, the R.S.F.S.R. Council of Ministers "ordered the Leningrad Sovnarkhoz, ministries, and departments of the R.S.F.S.R. to transfer to the stock of the local soviets the housing under the control of enterprises, organizations, and institutes in Leningrad."[7] At the same time, the housing-management organizations and funds were also taken over by the city. Almost a year before the actual decision had been made, from the beginning of 1965, plans were being laid to receive the additional housing. The amount transferred was about 3 million square meters of housing space, representing about one sixth of the city's housing. This raised the city's share of housing space to 87 per cent. Thus, Leningrad became the first Soviet city to realize the goal of bringing all housing (except for such special housing as university dormitories, cooperatives, and individual housing) under the control of local government.

The basic units of housing management in Leningrad are the housing bureaus, which grew up rather haphazardly throughout the city, each controlling from 2,000 to 30,000 square meters of housing space. (See Table 24.) In 1939, there had been 3,683 housing bureaus; by 1945, the number had been reduced to 2,470, and by 1956, to 1,164. Then, in 1959, the system was rationalized and consolidated. The number of housing bureaus

was reduced from 1,178 to about 350 and they were, as
much as possible, centered in a microrayon. It is
claimed that this has significantly reduced the cost
of management.   In a 1956 study of seven Leningrad
rayons, it was estimated that as a result of the
consolidation of housing bureaus, 416 administrative personnel were released and 615,000 rubles
saved.[8] The housing bureaus are directly responsible to the housing-management department in each
rayon.   In turn, the rayon department is under the
central direction of the Housing-Management Department of the city. Attached to the housing bureaus
are administrators, maintenance personnel, and
repairmen for minor work. The more complicated
repairs (for example, elevator repairs) are contracted out to local repair trusts.

Although the city is the administrator, the
basic standards for maintenance of housing are
centrally determined by the Republic Ministry of
Communal Economy, and most of the work is done by
research institutes attached to this ministry.   In
recent years, the ministry has been trying to
develop a detailed set of norms for all housing in
order to provide uniform standards of maintenance.
This task has not proved easy, because existing
housing stock comprises buildings of many different
types, ages, and states of repair. Seven basic
groups with subgroups were established, but housing
administrators admit that, apart from such broad
standards as the number of people to clean walks
and stairs, the norms have not been successful.
In effect, the standard of maintenance depends on
the local bureau, and in practice the conditions
vary widely. Nevertheless, in spite of the limita-
tion of central control which this result implies,
the Ministry of Communal Economy and especially
its institute doggedly proceed to look for universal standards which can somehow be enforced. It is
never suggested that the system be decentralized,
that the city be allowed to set standards, nor that
controls be put entirely into the hands of the
tenants (including the power to fire or penalize
personnel at will).

The research institutes have also been experimenting with ways to bring costs of current maintenance down to within the amount of rent collected. This task is not easy, given the generally low level of maintenance which has been characteristic in the past. The only feasible area in which reductions can be made is personnel. By Western standards, the number of maintenance and administrative personnel does appear excessive. The first step has been the consolidation of housing bureaus to reduce administrative personnel, which in Leningrad accounted for 65 per cent of the administrative expenses. The next step, which is now being discussed in the literature, is the complete elimination of the dezhurnii. The number has already been cut down considerably. Dezhurnii are similar to the Western concierge or superintendent; they oversee general maintenance and the security of public buildings. Another means of reducing personnel currently being stressed is automation of elevators and mechanization of maintenance. But there is a general shortage of new elevators of all types, and a general lack of funds and equipment to mechanize maintenance presents other problems. Thus, the twig broom and the shovel are still the basic implements.

Next to the lack of funds, the most serious shortcoming in housing maintenance is the lack of skilled personnel. Reports indicate that at least one and one half to two times the present number of skilled workers are needed for current repairs. A study that was made of Oktiabrskii Rayon in Leningrad (with housing offices employing 900 workers) indicated that only 10 per cent of bureau heads had middle or higher education; of 230 so-called engineers, only 45 had advanced qualifications; of 29 bookkeepers, only 23 had finished middle education.[9] A worker in the housing bureau is near the bottom of the social and wage scale.

Unable to find adequate and enforceable maintenance norms, a variety of other methods is

used to try raising the level of maintenance in
housing. Both trade unions and local government
agencies do extensive spot checking of buildings.
One section of inspectors from the Organization-
Instruction Department deals exclusively with
housing. The city Bureau of Technical Inventory
checks on costs and payments made in the housing
sector as does the Department of Cost and Distribution of Housing attached to the city Executive Committee. In 1963, the oblast trade-union
council created special worker committees in the
larger rayons of Leningrad to check on housing.
An interdepartmental subcommittee on housing of
the Executive Committee includes representatives
of both government and trade unions. Serious attention is also given to the tenants' complaints
by the deputies to local soviets, and apparently
they are partially successful in remedying the
worst conditions. Formal complaints can run as
high as 5,000 a year in one rayon. Finally,
yearly socialist competitions are held among
housing bureaus with prizes of 500 and 1,000
rubles given to those bureaus that maintain the
highest standards. The sum of all these devices
is fragmented control in which it is difficult to
place ultimate responsibility to oversee housing
management. But even the best system of checks
would be of little value with the problems of insufficient funds and trained personnel. One
partial solution has been organization of the
tenants for volunteer work.

HOUSING COMMITTEES

     The basic communication channel between local
government and the population is through the housing bureaus and the public-housing committees
chosen from among the inhabitants. Under city
supervision, each housing bureau organizes a
housing committee. The committee is composed of
seven to twenty-five members, elected for a two-
year term, in a general meeting of the inhabitants
in the microrayon by a show of hands. The

chairman of the housing committee is confirmed by
the _rayon_ soviet. The head of the housing bureau
works closely with the committee. The chairmen of
the local parents' committee, people's court, and
fire-security committee serve as ex officio committee members when they are not regular members.
The committee organizes various subcommittees on
such matters as finances, public services, culture,
mass affairs, sanitation, and so forth. A member
of the housing committee serves as the chairman of
the subcommittee, while the subcommittee members
are drawn from activists in the population. Be-
neath the housing committee and housing bureau,
each building with more than three families has
one responsible citizen, _otvetstvennii_, appointed
by the housing bureau on recommendation of the
inhabitants and approved by the housing committee.
The _otvetstvennii_ oversees the maintenance of the
building and disciplines the tenants. The housing
bureau, without going to court, can back up the
enforcement of regulations by the _otvetstvennii_
through tenant fines of up to 10 rubles.

The tasks of the housing committee are numerous. It investigates complaints, assists in col-
lecting rents and utilities charges, and oversees
the operations of the housing bureau. But even
more important are its tasks of mass agitation and
mobilization. Each housing bureau spends 1-2 per
cent of its income for mass cultural work.
Through the housing committee, this money is spent
on wall newspapers, propaganda literature, children's playgrounds, organization of youth and
sports activities, lectures, and so forth. The
housing committee is also responsible for organizing tenants for such special work as planting
trees and cleanup projects in the immediate area
and in the city at large. Also active at this
level of mass agitation are the trade union and
Party organizations. They work closely with the
housing committees, and Party members are expected
to take a leading role in the work of the committees. For example, it is usually a member of
the Party who lives in the building and serves as
otvetstvennii.

Housing committees are also supported and aided by local councils of deputies, in addition to the Party. Since the mid-1950's, deputies to the various local soviets living within the territory of a single housing management have been organized under a chairman to help in mass activities, to conduct inspections, and to deal with special problems. The city's Organization-Instruction Department helps to organize their activities.

ALLOCATION OF HOUSING

Responsibility for allocation of new housing and exchange of housing only partially rests with the housing bureaus, in order to prevent collusion and bribery of local housing officials. The housing bureau receives applications and keeps records, but the trade unions are primarily responsible for allocation of new housing, and the city operates a separate Bureau for Exchange of Housing Space. Currently, a person who already has housing space can only apply for new space if his family has less than 4.5 square meters per person. Priority is given to veterans and their widows and children, invalids, and servicemen. All applications for additional and new housing are investigated and approved by the trade unions before being leased by the Department of Housing Management. Various public committees also investigate the allocation, and there is little evidence of dishonesty in the distribution. The inequity in apartment space develops as a result of the increase and decrease in the size of families and the allocation of additional space to holders of such premium positions as directors, chairmen, professors, or possessors of higher degrees.

Exchange of apartments was initially transacted informally at certain street corners on Sunday mornings, but recently the city has taken over. Those who want to change can advertise for an exchange in a periodical bulletin put out by

the Bureau for the Exchange of Housing Space. The
number of exchanges is about 20,000-25,000 a year,
which constitutes less than 1 per cent annual
turnover of apartments.

CONCLUSION

Housing administration in Leningrad is a
sprawling problem that touches on the key issues
of local government. It involves the question of
continued expansion and progress, the delicate
relationship between local needs and desires and
central authorities of the republic and All-Union
Governments, widescale coordination at the city
and rayon level, relations with the masses, and
problems of satisfying the primary interests of
the population. Although it is claimed that the
ideology and the formal structure provide all the
necessary means to guide these activities and ac-
complish assigned goals, in reality extra means
and channels have had to be found. Through the
periods of rapid industrialization in the 1930's,
the 900-day siege of World War II, and the push for
reconstruction, Leningrad housing administrators
and the population, by their separate efforts and
with minimum materials and money, have somehow
managed to provide all citizens with minimal
housing, free from most of the hazards of the
elements. Ideology, except for the patriotism and
revolutionary enthusiasm of the citizenry, was of
little value in this task. In the mid-1950's, the
decision to expand housing space by 6-8 per cent a
year for the next two decades raised even more
problems of coordinating, organizing, and dealing
with the central authorities. The central government's great interest in this task proved a major
obstacle, because it meant a complex maze of
formal organizations with decrees and central
directives. The structure proved too fragmented
and complex for the task, and in practice the city
leaders had to find their own way. They set up a
small inner cabinet to deal with the problem and
included the head of the Architect-Planning

Department, the chairman of the Executive Committee
assisted by the vice-chairman in charge of the
construction departments, and usually the city
Party's first secretary. During 1957-64, the
chairman of the Leningrad Sovnarkhoz (economic
region) or his deputy also worked with this group.
This inner cabinet is well equipped to deal with
the central authorities and to mobilize local
forces and,when necessary, can include various
departments and coordinating committees that deal
with construction. The administrative coordinators
that deal with the details are the bureaus of the
Architect-Planning Department and its head,
V. Kamenskii, who assumes the over-all, major
direction of construction.

Because capital funds for construction are
allocated by the republic, the city does not have
to find its own capital resources, except those
needed to extend certain services and to establish
certain special housing projects. Nevertheless,
city leaders, particularly the members of the
Architect-Planning Department, are under constant
pressure to find ways to reduce construction time,
costs, and labor. They also must help the construction trusts and combinats in obtaining a constant flow of materials. Each quarter, they must
assure the completion of the required number of
housing units according to the plan. As indicated
by frequent articles in the press and professional
journals, the Architect-Planning Department would
also like to assure adequate quality standards, but
this is still something for the future. As a
result of prodigious efforts, there has been an
increase of almost 75 per cent in the amount of
housing space in the city of Leningrad, since the
mid-1950's.

NOTES TO CHAPTER 5

1. Arkhitektura S. S. S. R. [Architecture
U.S.S.R.], No. 12 (1965), p. 3.

2. Stroitelstvo i arkhitektura Leningrada
[Construction and Architecture of Leningrad], No. 9
(1965), p. 18.

3. One study estimated the following average
costs and time for construction:

Individual brick apartments: 148.7 rubles
per square meter, 11 to 12 months; large block apartments: 126.6 rubles per square meters, 8 to 9
months; large panel apartments: 115.2 rubles per
square meter, 5 to 5 1/2 months.

Sh. M. Ginzburg, Ekonomika krupnopanelnogo
domostroiniia [The Economics of Large Panel Housing
Construction] (Moscow, 1962), pp. 6-7.

4. Stroitelslvo i Architektura Leningrada
[Construction and Architecture of Leningrad] (July,
1964), p. 15.

5. In the case of buildings costing 100,000-
200,000 rubles, for example, the city as consumer
comes directly into the building process only at
the final stages when 1-2 per cent of the cost
remains to be paid. For buildings over 200,000
rubles, the consumer has a chance to participate
after about 90 per cent of the cost has been paid.

6. In the R.S.F.S.R., the basic rent for
living space is 3.5-4.4 kopecks per square meter.
For each ruble a worker earns over 14.5 rubles per
month, he pays an additional .33 kopecks up to
13.2 kopecks for one square meter of living space.
For apartments built since the 1920's, a local
soviet may charge 25 per cent more. The basic
norm is 9 square meters per person, with an additional 4.5 square meters for each family. For

any space above the norm, a tenant must pay triple
rent. If the tenant has 4 dependents, there is a
5 per cent reduction in rent; for 5 dependents,
10 per cent; and for 6 or more dependents, 15 per
cent. Additional reductions are made for dark or
otherwise undesirable space.

7. Biulleten Ispolkoma Lengorsoveta [Bulletin
of the Executive Committee of the Leningrad City
Soviet], No. 20 (1965), p. 5.

8. Gorodskoe khoziaistvo, (Leningrad, 1957),
p. 30.

9. In the Soviet Union the bookkeeper has a
double role. He must keep the records and audit
and oversee the fulfillment of the plan on behalf
of higher authorities.

CHAPTER 6 PROBLEMS AND PROSPECTS FOR THE FUTURE

The insular tendencies of the Soviet Union, the restricted development of consumer goods, and a centralized, authoritarian regime have created a system of local government in Leningrad quite unique from the pattern found in the non-Communist world. But the factors leading to this state of affairs have been changing gradually. The Soviet Union is no longer as isolated from outside influence, consumer goods have assumed a new priority, and attempts are being made to rationalize and clarify responsibility at the local level. Thus, it is reasonable to assume that in the future Leningrad will face not only its own unique problems, but problems more closely related to those of cities in the non-Communist world.

In discussing prospects for the future, it must again be stressed that compared to other Soviet cities, Leningrad is in a favorable position. The major problems that face most Soviet cities, such as an irrational division of communal services between local government and separate enterprises, the difficulty of coordinating local-government activities with central authorities and enterprises in the local area, and red tape in getting crucial decisions out of Moscow, are present in Leningrad, but to a lesser degree. There has always been a more rational division of functions between the city and the organs of the national economy in Leningrad, and this was strengthened when almost all housing was turned over to city management in 1965. Furthermore, the prestige of

the city and its leaders gives them greater access
to central authorities and their conflicts are
settled more quickly. So, in addition to the problems discussed below, other cities in the Soviet
Union face a difficult and persistent problem of
relating quickly and efficiently to central authorities and independent local enterprises.

ADMINISTRATIVE PROBLEMS

In order to impose a totalitarian regime on
the Soviet people, the leadership has tended to
sacrifice organizational stability and rationality
for flexibility and responsiveness to orders from
above and to the central government's priority interests. For the city of Leningrad, this has
meant, first of all, a rapid turnover of personnel,
both planned and unplanned. At the upper echelons
of city administration, such turnover is planned
as a means of preventing so-called family power
groups from developing. It is also planned so
that the most talented leaders at the local level
are promoted and even drafted to work in Moscow.
This includes Party and government administrators,
educators, scientists, and artists. It is difficult for Leningrad to maintain its status as a
cultural, scientific, and educational center when
the real future for its talented youth is in Moscow.
The unplanned turnover of personnel is primarily in
the lower echelons and is due to the low status and
income of city employees compared to those in heavy
industry. The most serious consequence of the turnover is not so much the inefficiency of the administrative system--which is considerable--but lack
of initiative, reluctance to alter routines, and
the low quality of services and goods.

Closely associated with reducing the turnover
of personnel to improve local administration is
the need to divide responsibility and functions
rationally. Unfortunately, Khrushchev's decentralization scheme adopted in 1957 proved to be ill-
conceived and poorly planned and administered.

Confusion, rivalry, and localism were the results.
As a consequence, his successors have recentralized
the powers that he had given to economic regions;
in some areas, such as construction, finance, and
materials, central direction has even been strengthened. Nevertheless, the decentralization of power
to the republics has been maintained, because the
actions of the republics can still easily be controlled. Furthermore, the Baltic republics, and to
a lesser extent, Belo Russia and the Ukraine, proved
their superior administrative efficiency during
the period of decentralization. Also, as autonomous units, they are useful for experimentation
with new administrative techniques. Some of the
central Asian republics, however, continue to require special tutelage. Finally, the government
of the R.S.F.S.R., which is by far the most important republic, is housed in Moscow along with the
All-Union Government and the two are closely integrated. Within the vast Russian Republic, there
are no signs thus far of even a cautious return to
greater autonomy, although this step would seem to
be essential to a rationalization of the system.
On the contrary, by applying computers and formulas,
the so-called scientists in the central research
institutes are trying to find absolute standards
for housing, communal services, public catering,
and employee initiative. Rarely do the writers in
the professional journals, even in passing, mention decentralization. The articles are full of
new formulas. It is, however, significant that
almost all the examples of successful and advanced
standards which are cited in the journals come
from Belo Russia and the Baltic republics. The
territory and population of all four of these republics are small, and they each have only one
large, major urban center of less than 1 million
to supervise.

But even though centralized authority has re-
turned to its pre-Khrushchev state, there have
been cautious steps at rationalizing the distribution of functions at the local level. Thus, housing management and trade in Leningrad, discussed

earlier, are now more concentrated under the city's administration, rather than diversified among various organizations. Also, in the field of security, the local militia and other organs of public order work more closely with the city. At the same time, the coordinating function of the city government has been greatly expanded so that the various departments at least have an idea of what other departments are doing. There is a strong tendency in a totalitarian society for administrators to put on blinders and concentrate on their own narrow task, to avoid being involved in the problems and perhaps the criminal failures of the other departments. Although Soviet propaganda has stressed the over-all responsibility of each local government administrator for all departments, in practice administrators have avoided this joint responsibility and resisted even knowing what was going on in the neighboring department. From our interviews, it is clear this attitude still largely prevails.

Resistance to broad responsibility also developed as a result of the welter of checks and watchdogs on every government administrator. The Party, the people's control commissions, trade unions, the Department of Finance, banks, Gosplan, the Organization-Instruction Department, inspectors from departments and central ministries, permanent city and rayon commissions, and various activist groups are all primary investigators of local government. In some cases, such as housing, all of these groups are active. Nevertheless, by their own admission, these groups are not successful, and the system of supervision is too fragmented to be effective. In the specific case of the trade unions and citizens' groups, investigation is often a meaningless matter of form. In other cases, the organs are looking at total production or one specific production index, for which they require a formal fulfillment. Even in those cases where over-all quality is investigated, as for example by the inspectors of the Architect-Planning Department, little can be done besides giving the matter publicity. Additional resources needed to raise quality standards, as well as disciplinary action, must come from Moscow and these rarely seem forthcoming except in cases of gross negligence. Thus, the system requires simpler and more meaningful lines of responsibility. Additional resources, less stress on production and more on quality seem to be essential.

The Soviet Union has not as yet come up with a system of incentives that will encourage quality and initiative, but for the first time, the Soviet Union and other countries of the Communist bloc are talking about the problem and exploring solutions. Soviet experiments, thus far, have been the most conservative and cautious and it is more likely that another Eastern European country will first produce a workable solution. Nevertheless, the recent reform allowing retail trade organizations to order directly from producers as needed and to sell goods as demanded seems to be the first direct move to give the public positive influence over consumer items, in contrast to ineffective protection by numerous investigating and controlling bodies. A conflict remains between proponents of improved central quality indexes and advocates of consumer demands as solutions to the quality problem. If the current leadership's cautious policy of experimentation is followed, it would seem likely that both approaches will be used and reform will be slow.

SOCIAL PROBLEMS

Like most large cities today, Leningrad has had increasing juvenile delinquency. Crime statistics are not published, nor are they made available to the researcher in the Soviet Union, but from the number of articles on the subject in the local and national press, it is clear that Leningrad has not escaped this problem. Soviet writers tend to blame the Western influence, with its beatniks, long hair, blue jeans, and rock and roll. While Western influences certainly set the mode of the juvenile

revolt, the problem is deeper. The repudiations of
Stalin, then Beria, Malenkov, and Khrushchev have
shattered the illusions and idealism of Soviet
youth.   In addition, the gradual infiltration of
new ideas from outside and the growing doubts about
achievement of the Communist utopia have resulted
in a significant decline of adherence to ideology
among all ages, but particularly among teenagers
and young adults. As a result, the stale slogans
and the strongly politicized culture and recreation
organized by the Komsomols (Party youth organizations) have ceased to attract the respect and alle-
giance of youth. Furthermore, the small family
living areas inevitably mean that teenagers seek
activity in the streets and in gangs. But Leningrad at least does not have the complicating factor
of school dropouts. Every child must finish the
ten-year school, and if he is not qualified or interested in going on, there is a job waiting for him

The major response of the city and other author
ities to this hooliganism of youth has been largely
repression. Lip service is given to the idea of
more creative work among youth, but the evidence
generally indicates that old patterns are being re-
peated. The curfew on youth is rigidly enforced,
as are restrictions on drinking. The spontaneous
clubs that spring up from time to time among university students and others are forcibly dissolved.
The citizens' committees for public order
(druzhini)   and militia are mobilized to keep
hooligans off the street and to disperse street
gangs. Parents are made responsible for the activities of their children. As a result, at least
on the surface, the problem seems to be in hand,if
not solved, and violence from teenage gangs is not
widespread.

In other areas of typical urban social problems, Leningrad is more fortunate. It has few
minorities and none are distinctive. There is virtually no unemployment. In fact, there is generally a labor shortage. With automation, most of the
unskilled jobs are being eliminated, but the

changeover is gradual enough so that the natural
retirement of the older, unskilled workers is sufficient to absorb the technological change without
putting people out of work. In the postwar period,
there was a large number of squatter shacks around
Leningrad, but the expansion of new housing since
the 1950's has largely absorbed these settlements.

Less than 4 per cent of the city's population
is over sixty years of age, so that the aged and
retired are not as yet a serious problem in Leningrad. Over half of those above retirement age are
on pensions. Those not on pensions are supported by
families and very few are wards of the city. Even
pensioners usually find that their pensions are
meager and continue to work in cloakrooms or as
concierges. The most serious problem in connection
with the aged, which also affects the population
as a whole, is the lack of hospital space. In
1953, there were 33,100 beds; by 1963, this had increased to 41,300, but the number is still inadequate, and many bedridden and senile people who
need hospitalization have to be cared for by families in crowded accommodations.

PLANNING PROBLEMS

The absence of a large suburban development
and the ownership of all land by the government
without any monetary value being attached to it has
permitted city planners to draft a comprehensive
plan of development with large parks and recreational areas. Inherently, there is little to keep
these plans from being carried out and enforced.
The two major conditional factors are the willingness of the central government to continue to allocate necessary capital funds for industry and housing and the continued growth of population. A
serious decline of Leningrad's population growth
in the 1960's may force alteration of the city's
general plan, and Leningrad may again be eclipsed
by more rapidly growing areas.

New housing, as discussed in Chapter 5, is adequate, but the monotony and poor quality of the construction are likely to create future problems. Of more immediate concern, however, is the problem of urban renewal. Even in the areas of no histori- cal interest in Leningrad, old buildings are rarely razed but are repaired when they have deteriorated to less than 50 per cent of their original useful- ness. This repair often costs as much or more than new construction, and the results are often unsat- isfactory. The economics of capital repair are only beginning to be challenged, and as yet, little has been done in Leningrad to consider or plan major projects of urban renewal through razing and planning new construction.

Another unresolved problem that may have the most serious consequences on the future of Lenin- grad is that of private automobile transportation. With emphasis on consumer goods and the growing buying power of the population, pressure for more automobiles began to develop in the mid-1950's. Malenkov and even Khrushchev made some general promises to increase automobile production. Then, in the early 1960's, Khrushchev changed his mind, held back production, and almost doubled the price of private cars. The new Soviet leadership appears to have cautiously reversed that decision. It has contracted for a Fiat plant in the Soviet Union and plans to increase the production of Soviet automobiles as well. The general plan of Lenin- grad, however, is predicated on the increase of public transportation and makes no provision for large-scale private transport. Even today, with only commercial traffic, some of the streets in the center area are overburdened. Thus, if there is a marked increase in the number of private automobiles, and it is doubtful that the regime can resist such a development, traffic and parking will become the number one problem in Leningrad. New planning and major investments in expressways will be necessary. Surprisingly, Moscow has al- ready taken some important steps in this direction, but in Leningrad, except for some very general articles on the subject, nothing has been done.

In conclusion, Leningrad is only beginning to face the social and economic problems which have overwhelmed many Western metropolises. And in spite of the greater authority and planning in the Soviet system, it is doubtful that Soviet local administrators have a greater capability of solving these problems than city officials elsewhere.

BIBLIOGRAPHY

BIBLIOGRAPHY

Books and Monographs

Altunin, S. E., et al. Kooperativnoe zhilishchnoe
    stroitelstvo v. Leningrade. Leningrad: 1964.

Azovkin, I. A. Organizatsiia raboti v ispolkome
    raionnovo soveta. Moscow: 1959.

Bachilo, I. L. Rol mestnikh organov gosundarstvennii
    vlasti v razvitii narodnovo obrazovaniia i
    kulturi. Moscow: 1959.

Balmakova, I. K., et al. Finansirovanie i rascheti
    v zhilishchnom stroitelstve, osushchestvliaemom
    silami. Leningrad and Moscow: 1961.

Berezov, V. A. V partiinuiu rabotu--obshchestvennie
    nachala. Leningrad: 1964.

Bezuglov, A. A. Glasnost raboti mestnikh sovetov.
    Moscow: 1960.

Bibliotechka deputata mestnovo soveta. Moscow:
    1960.

Broner, D. L. Sovremennie problemi zhilishchnovo
    khoziaistva. Moscow: 1961.

Dmitriev, N. G., and Rozantsev, C. H. Spravochnik
    po zhilishchnim voprocam. Moscow: 1963.

Ekspluatatsiia i kapitalnii remont zhilikh zdanii.
    Moscow and Leningrad: 1962.

Ekonomika stroitelstva i gorodskovo khoziaistva.
Leningrad: 1965.

Eropkin, M.I. Uchastie trudiashchikhsia v
okhrane obshchestvennovo poriadka. Moscow:
1959.

Fedorov, I. L. Pravovoe polozhenie sovetov
narodnovo khoziaistva. Moscow: 1960.

Filinovich, Iu. K. Sovetskii deputat. Moscow:
1958.

Galperin, I. M., and Polozkov, F. A. Uchastie
obshchestvennosti v sovestskom ugolovnom
protsesse. Moscow: 1961.

Ginzburg, Sh. M. Ekonomika krupnopanelnogo
domostroeniia. Moscow: 1965.

Goncharov, A. Ia. Obshchestvennost i ispolnitelnii
komitet raionovo soveta. Moscow: 1960.

Gorod velikovo Lenina. Leningrad: 1957.

Goroda-sputniki (Sbornik statei). Moscow: 1961.

Gorodskoe khoziaistvo. Leningrad: 1957.

Goure, Leon. The Siege of Leningrad. Stanford:
Stanford University Press, 1962.

Gradstroitelnie problemi razvitie Leningrada.
Leningrad: 1960.

Iampolskaia, Ts. A., et al. Pravovie voprosi
organizatsii i deiatelnimi sovnarknozov.
Moscow: 1961.

Iuridicheskii spravochnik deputata mestnovo soveta.
Moscow: 1960.

Karasev, A. V. Leningradtsi v godi blokadi,
1941-1943. Moscow: 1959.

Kobalevskii, V. L., et al. Ekonomika i organizatsiia gorodskovo khoziaistva. Moscow: 1964.

Kosarevich, A. N. Sovetskaia obshchestvennost v borbe s prestupnostiu. Moscow: 1959.

Kotovoi, S. P., et al. Novoe v rabote mestnikh sovetov. Leningrad: 1961.

Kozlova, E. I. Ispolnitelnie comiteti gorodskikh sovetov deputatov trudiashchikhsia. Moscow: 1960.

KPSS. Leningradskaia organizatsiia. Leningrad: 1963.

Kratkii istocherk. Leningrad: 1964.

Leningrad. Leningrad: 1943.

Leningrad i Leningradskaia Oblast v tsifrakh. Leningrad: 1964.

Leningradskaia gor. konferentsiia po okhrane atmosfernovo vozdukha. Leningrad: 1963.

Likhanov, F. G. Proverka ispolneniia v rabote mestnikh sovetov deputatov trudiashchikhsia. Moscow: 1959

Lunev, A. E. Administrativnaia otvetstvennost za pravonarusheniia. Moscow: 1961.

Malshev, I. V. O roli narodnikh mass v sovetskom sotsialisticheskom obshchestve. Moscow: 1960.

Manakov, N., and Petrov, N. Gorodskoe khoziaistvo Leningrada. Leningrad: 1949.

O plane razvitiia gor. khoz. Len. Leningrad: 1962.

O 250-letii Leningrada. Leningrad: 1957.

Osnovin, V. S.   Postiannie komissii sotsialistiches
koi zakonnisti i okhranie obshchestvennovo
poriadka mestnikh sovetov. Moscow: 1960.

Petrovskii, I. I.   Postiannie komissii raikoma
partii. Leningrad: 1963.

Piskotin, M. I.   Biuzhetnie prava mestnikh sovetov
deputatov trudiashchikhsia. Moscow: 1961.

Polozheniia o postiannikh komissiakh mestnikh
sovetov deputatov trudiashchikhsia. Moscow:
1958.

Postnikov, M. A., and Shapovalov, V. S.   Porgotovka
i provedenie zasedanii ispolnitelnovo komiteta
raionnovo soveta deputatov trudiashchikhsia.
Moscow: 1959.

Pronina, V. S.   Rol mestnikh sovetov v del
preduprezhdeniia pravonarushenii nesover-
shennoletnikh. Moscow: 1961.

Safarov, R. A.   Raionnie soveti deputatov
trudiashchikhsia v gorodakh. Moscow: 1961.

Sbornik reshenii ispolkoma Lengorsoveta. Leningrad
1960.

Shchiglik, A. I.   Rol ispolnitelnikh komitetov v
organizatsionno-massovoi rabote. Khabarovsk:
1960.

Sobolev, A. I.   Roznichnaia torgovlia Leningrada i
perspektivi ee razvittia. Leningrad: 1963.

Spravochnik partiinovo rabotnika. Moscow: 1961.

Tikhomirov, Iu. A.   Mestnie soveti i sovnarkhozi.
Moscow: 1959.

Todorskii, Iu. V.   Postiannie komissii mestnikh
sovetov deputatov trudiashchikhsia. Moscow:
1955.

Uchastnie obshchestvennooti v rabote mestnikh
    sovetov (Sbornik documentov). Moscow: 1960.

Vakhanskii, E. Vlast narodnaia, soveti na puti k
    kommunisticheskomu samoupravleniiu. Lenin-
    grad: 1962.

Verizhnikov, S. M. Zhilishchnaia problema i podzem
    blagosostoianiia tradiashchikhsia Leningrada.
    Leningrad: 1962.

Vishniakov, V. G. Priem naselenia v ispolkomakh
    mestikh sovetov. Moscow: 1961.

Voprosi partiinovo stroitelstva (Sbornik statei).
    Leningrad: 1965.

Voprosi proizvoditelnosti truda i sebestoimosti v
    zhilishchnom stroitelstve. Leningrad: 1962.

Zhilishchnoe khoziaistvo (Sbornik statei). Moscow
    and Leningrad: 1964.

Zhilishchnoe stroitelstvo v SSSR. Moscow: 1963.

Periodicals

Arkhitektura S.S.S.R.

Biulleten Ispolnitelnovo Komiteta Leningradskovo
    Gorodskovo Soveta Deputatov Trudiashchikhsia.

Biulleten Ispolnitelnovo Komiteta Leningradskovo
    Oblastnovo Soveta.

Ekonomika stroitelstva.

Leningradskaia Pravda.

Soveti deputatov trudiashchikhsia.

Stroitelstvo i arkhitektura Leningrada.

Zhilishchno-kommunalnoe khoziaistvo.

ABOUT THE AUTHOR

David T. Cattell, a Professor of Political
Science at the University of California (Los
Angeles), has devoted most of his professional
life to study of the Soviet Union and other Com-
munist systems. He received a B.A. from Amherst
College and the Certificate of the Russian
Institute and a doctorate from Columbia University
in 1953. He has made four trips to the Soviet
Union, two of them to participate in exchange
programs at the University of Leningrad. Professor
Cattell has written numerous published articles
and is the author of Soviet Diplomacy and the
Spanish Civil War (1957), as well as Communism
and the Spanish Civil War (1955,1965).

The Institute of Public Administration, New
York, is a private, nonprofit educational and research institution. It is the oldest professional
center of its type in the United States, originally
founded as the New York Bureau of Municipal Research in 1906. Its work in recent years has been
focused on research and technical assistance on
government organization and policy problems and
urban and human resources development.